"Your personal brand is the public fingerprint you leave on the world."

ISAAC MASHMAN

Acclaim for Isaac Mashman

Winston Churchill famously stated, "Success consists of going from failure to failure without loss of enthusiasm." No one said entrepreneurship would be easy. No one told the phoenix to rise from its ashes; it was of its nature to emerge from the fire and fly. Isaac embodies this spirit of resilience, proving that grit and tenacity breed success.

> *- Kevin McDonald*
> *Isaac's Childhood Best Friend*

Isaac Mashman exemplifies the spirit of lifelong learning and leadership. As an alumnus of River City Science Academy, he has not only carved out a successful path in business and personal branding, but has also remained deeply engaged with the school community. Growing up in RCSA's diverse environment, he was exposed to different cultures, perspectives, and ways of thinking—an experience that has been instrumental in shaping his ability to understand and connect with people.

Seeing alumni like Isaac thrive and give back, fills me with immense pride. It is moments like these that make all the sacrifices and hard work worthwhile, reminding me that the impact of education extends far beyond the classroom. His journey is a testament to the power of resilience, vision, and giving back.

> *- Sel Buyuksarac*
> *Co-founder of River City Science Academy*

Isaac Mashman deserves a lot of praise for the way he makes you question your personal and professional branding. He does this at a high level that is yet very relatable to most individuals and entrepreneurs.

- Jeff Weemhoff
President of Atlantic-Oase

Branding isn't just about logos, colors, or clever taglines—it's about trust, authority, and authenticity. Isaac Mashman gets this at a level few do. In an industry flooded with surface-level gimmicks, Isaac stands out by leading with integrity, real expertise, and an obsession with results. He doesn't just build brands; he builds legacies. If you're not paying attention to what he's doing, you're already behind.

- Adrian Boysel
Friend and Mentor

Isaac Mashman is both an incredible businessman and friend. He has always been ready and able to help me out in my times of need and has gotten my branding to where it needs to be. Since our first meeting, he has remained an active part of my life.

- Tristan T. Roberts
Gold & Platinum Certified Engineer

PERSONAL BRANDING:

A Manifesto on Fame and Influence

— Second Edition —

Isaac Mashman

At the center of all achievement is personal growth.

- Isaac Mashman

| F |
Foreword
Written by Eric Chow

I certainly never expected that Personal Branding would become a key part of my life or professional career. It makes me wonder if Isaac would have predicted it would be such a critical part of his; and yet, as I look back on my life thus far, its usefulness to me *(and its drawbacks)* are apparent and obvious.

It was my personal brand as a great math student that led my former teacher to suggest that I should tutor on the subject. It ultimately became a strong source of income while I was in college. It was my reputation for authentic and insightful conversation that led me to host a podcast that was listened to in nearly 100 countries within 3 years. Likewise, it was my knack for networking that opened doors to host business and social events, foster relationships with mentors, travel, earn promotions, and more.

Beyond my skills, my personality and my character also mattered—the way I carried myself and treated others shaped the most fruitful friendships, while my flaws also led to difficult and even emotional ends to others. My reputation for the kind of man I was led to introductions, job and business opportunities, and referrals. My life has tremendously benefited and at times taken hits, due to my personal brand.

For nearly a decade, I have been obsessed with reading books on personal development, from business, communication, emotional intelligence, leadership, productivity, psychology, sales, wealth, and related genres. Amidst all of these discussions, your individual personal brand—your credibility, reputation, and ability to influence others—plays a pivotal role in your success, but it's rarely given the attention it deserves.

I recently picked up my old high school yearbook. As I flipped through the pages, I noticed two things almost simultaneously. First, I remembered people. My experiences with them and what I had recently seen on their social media, influenced my reactions. As I read their names and saw their pictures, I recalled some of them with fondness, others with disappointment, and for many, I simply wondered what had become of them and where they were in life. Second, I saw their notes about me—my reputation for being academic and studious, my personality, and my ethos. Of course, a yearbook only includes the positive notes, so it also made me wonder what they would have previously said about my faults.

Our personal brand is the recognition our name gets, what we're associated with, and the reputation it carries in terms of character and credibility. Who we are, what we do and how well we do it, the way we carry ourselves, and how we treat others all affect how we are remembered—if at all. What we share about ourselves, online and otherwise, is a continued expression of that.

In a world where anybody can have a platform and information is abundant, what separates us is our *"personal brand."* More specifically, that unique combination of our *"person"* and our *"brand."*
But what does that entail?

That's what *A Manifesto on Fame and Influence* is all about.

So, what is your goal?

- Fame and popularity?
- Being followed and in demand in your field?
- Making money?
- Being known as an expert, innovator, leader, or visionary?

- Landing your dream job or promotion?
- Leading a phenomenal team?
- Positively impacting a community?
- Attracting investors?
- Finding your dream partner in life?
- Getting to work with your favorite brands as an ambassador?
- Owning a successful business?
- Getting elected into public office?

Regardless of what it is you are pursuing, along with the skills that are required to do well, your ability to intentionally and strategically direct your own personal brand, credibility, and reputation will be a key factor in your success.

It was August 11th, 2019. Two days before, I had spontaneously decided to launch *The Eric Chow Empowers Podcast,* a show that would later have listeners in 96 countries around the world before I ended it. I was on Twitter, or X as it is now called, when I saw this tweet by a man I had been following for a few months: *"I'm looking to go on a podcast tour!"* Being a new podcaster, I shot my shot.

Imagine my surprise when it worked! Isaac Mashman, a few short hours later, gave me his phone number. Years later, Isaac and I found ourselves working together, consulting clients and developing our philosophy and tools on personal branding. We were honing our skills as businessmen in a venture that later led Isaac to publish the First Edition of *Personal Branding: A Manifesto on Fame and Influence,* and eventually, the creation of Mashman Consulting Group.

While I believe any notable business leader, entertainer, influencer, professional, or politician, would acknowledge the importance of having a following, solid credibility, and a stellar reputation, few possess Isaac's depth of understanding on the subject. The analogy that comes to mind is this: if we brush and floss our teeth for good oral hygiene, why are there dentists? Isaac is that expert.

I've witnessed firsthand Isaac's insightful perspective. Countless times, he's encountered content—an article, podcast, or video discussing personal branding. He would then offer his own analysis, acknowledging valid points while often revealing a more nuanced, compelling perspective. I'm confident you'll have the same experience as you read and digest this book.

The Second Edition is a far more thorough deep-dive into the intricacies, principles, strategies, and often not-thought-about challenges of building a far-reaching and long-lasting personal brand. Regardless of the scale in which you decide to build your own, contemplate what it means to have an unrivaled personal brand and how you might define success.

If this man from Union City, California can be so bold, I believe this book will evolve to be the *Think and Grow Rich* and *How to Win Friends & Influence People* on personal branding—THE differentiator in the 21st century.

Eric Chow
@ericchowreal

Dedicated to YOU, the singular person that this Manifesto talks about.

This is the world's first *"Philosophy of Personal Branding"* with practical guiding principles.

| P |

Insights

I | **About The Second Edition**

The Second Edition of Isaac Mashman's *Personal Branding: A Manifesto on Fame and Influence* is a continuation and remarkably more mature look into personal branding. It is in-depth as it is practical, while concomitantly presenting philosophical and psychological approaches that would be atypical of other definitions of the era. The Second Edition contains tactics found in principle that will extend past the current day and age.

It is its principled nature that will prevent it from becoming obsolete in the years to come when held against similar publications. Isaac has provided a firm blueprint and foundation that anyone can use to develop their understanding and scale their personal brand into something that serves them in the pursuit of their ambitions.

This edition is compartmentalized into chapters and subchapters to help with organization and for your future reference; with an index of terms being found at the end. The main chapters are as follows: *Education, Branding, Reputation Management,*

Marketing, *Personal Skills*, *Identity Positioning*, and *Sustainability*.

There are nearly 80 *subchapters* in total, and at the end of each you will notice that there are several kinds of exercises. **Questions** are demarcated as "**Q:**" **Tasks** are demarcated as **"T:"** and tasks you are to **Apply** are labeled with **"A:."** These are not required, but it is highly recommended to increase retention and inspire creative thinking. Complete each of these to the best of your ability, and have a notebook as a companion if you do not want to directly write in the book.

If you choose to reread this Manifesto at any point, take the time to complete each activity again as you will find your answers and efforts to have evolved. Certain strategies may also become more apparent and although the text itself didn't change, you as the reader will.

II | From The Author, Second Edition

I would like to extend a warm and cordial welcome to each person who picks up the Second Edition of *Personal Branding: A Manifesto on Fame and Influence*. This will be one of the most important books you will ever read IF you apply the principles and strategies I unveil, and IF you open your mind to just how powerful your personal brand actually is. You can change the world with your words, and could change the face of corporations and others with your endorsements.

The publication of the Second Edition comes a little over 3 years after that of the First. I originally said that I would likely never publish another book on the subject of personal branding. Needless to say, things change. As it pertains to my Manifesto, I believe I have opened the door to writing expanded editions in the future, similar to that of textbooks or the various *legacy* works we find ourselves coming back to. I have included insights into what the Third Edition will be in the *Afterword*.

Almost immediately after the First Edition's publication, I found myself rereading it. I wasn't searching for grammatical or spelling errors, for that

I am proud of, but I was rereading it with the hope that I would find some sort of hidden knowledge.

My intent was never to have the most strategic compilation on the subject of personal branding; rather I intended to establish what personal branding is, why you should be building your personal brand, and to change the perception surrounding it. Now that I have had the opportunity to share my definition which I believe to be backed by evidence and have empirically proved by practical examination, I am emboldened enough to say that with the publication of my expanded Manifesto, I have established the world's first *Philosophy of Personal Branding*. Yes, I have included strategies, but I want to set the core tenets of belief and the standards of practice.

There isn't a School of Personal Branding, nor some governing body or organization that adds structure to the subject like that of the bar exam or becoming a practicing doctor. I will use my Manifesto to attempt to fill in the gaps that would otherwise be set by formal institutions. Edward Bernays himself, the father of public relations, nephew to Sigmund Freud, and consultant to American Presidents Woodrow Wilson, Calvin Coolidge, Herbert Hoover, and Dwight D.

Eisenhower, talked about the flaws of the space he helped create in interviews from later in his life.

As an early adopter and professional in the personal branding space, I am taking a similar stance and hope to make this Manifesto and my statements the backbone for future professionals.

I often joke that if I had attended secondary education, if not for marketing, I would have pursued a degree in Psychology. I was complimented on the psychology found in the First Edition, but my aim is even deeper here with you now.

After each chapter and subchapter, think of similar situations that you have been in that correlate with the provided information, and prove these concepts to yourself with evidence from within your own life. I am confident that you will find this Manifesto to contain a high degree of accuracy.

This text is not meant to be read once and left on the table or bookshelf to collect dust. Sit with a separate pen, paper, highlighter, and consider recording your thoughts in real time so you can truly digest what I have written. I would discourage you from attempting to read this all in one sitting.

Treat this more along the lines of a textbook that you would study, although I doubt you will find it as boring as one. I'd also like to mention that the word *"you"* and its derivatives are used nearly, if not in excess of 3,000 times. More than anything, this is a book about YOU. Personal branding has existed since the beginning of humankind and the principles that I share will stand true regardless of technology, forms of media, and the current state of civilization. We have all read books that only applied for the first few years after publication. My biggest fear is to write something that is relevant today, and irrelevant tomorrow.

Much love,
Isaac Mashman

CONTENTS

3. Mindset

8 Subchapters

4. Branding

16 Subchapters

5. Reputation Management
14 Subchapters

6. Marketing
12 Subchapters

7. Personal Skills

6 Subchapters

i. Identity Positioning   295

Essay *Identity Positioning: A Macroscopic View on Personal Branding*

8. Sustainability

10 Subchapters

PERSONAL BRANDING

Opening Words

What if there was something so powerful that you could get nations to do your bidding, millions of people to follow you, and be able to have a direct impact on the world's future landscape?

To have the ability to get people to do what you tell them to do, resulting in fame, influence, riches, and power. To be remembered in times well past your life. A concept that can be used both for good and for bad, the definitions of which are up for your interpretation. A concept that can drive a mission forward and bring awareness to a cause, so much so that people are waking up asking what they can do to support it. What if I told you that this concept is not as far-fetched and distant as you might think?

If I told you that you too, can tap into the benefits of this concept, would you believe me? Whether you believe me or not, frankly does not matter. It still exists. This concept has been a part of *us* since the beginning of intelligent man and will forever be ingrained in our nature.

What I am discussing is known as *personal branding*. Throughout this work, I will do my best to tactfully explain what personal branding is, why you should be building yours, how public figures throughout history have become the people we now study, and the ways in which you can preserve and guide your individual reputation. It is a manual that teaches you how you can pave a path of legitimate fame and influence that parallels that of your idols.

It does not require you to spend millions of dollars on external resources, as what you need, you already possess, nor does it require you to want to become famous or influence millions. It applies to the stay at home parent or student out of middle school as much as it does the next business mogul or international icon.

The largest selling point and competitive advantage made available is YOU.

Your personal brand.

| 1 |

Education

The foundation and understanding needed to fully comprehend the chapters to come

1.1 | **What Is Personal Branding?**

If you asked me to summarize the concept of personal branding in one word, I would simply reply with *"You."* In its truest, most holistic form it is you. Who you are, what people know you for, and the distinctive combination of characteristics and personality traits that only you possess. The totality of your life experiences, your hobbies, your interests, your passions, and even your fears. All of your successes and all of your failures. Your lessons and your shortcomings. All of it is compiled under your personal brand.

As someone who has been in the business world for all of my adult life, I have witnessed one misconception being made time and time again. It is the misnomer that a company brand is the same as a personal brand. When you're launching a business, you have to give it certain traits, decide on its brand colors and their psychological implications, and go out of your way to make it known what your business is and what it offers.

In contrast, *one does not give themself a personal brand, as it has already existed.* For proper representation, they should determine what they want to be seen as in the public's eye and make decisions that will have a positive contribution to their overall reputation. Personal brand and company brand are two separate entities that should be built correlatively. It also applies to other use cases such as authors and their books, podcasters and their podcasts, and movie stars and their movies. They are not their forms of media; their media are extensions of them.

Whether you are leveraging the internet or going out to brunch to network, there must be a firm distinction between this is *"me,"* and this is my body of work. It applies not only to the business owner but to all other niches. The end goal of making your personal brand attractive enough so that opportunities seek you out, remains the same. To be sought after for a series of publicly vindicated reasons.

Imagine that you have a personal promoter tagging along 24/7. This promoter is talking about how great you are, is sharing your accomplishments, running advertisements, and doing everything in their power to propel you forward. *This promoter is your personal brand.* You could be sleeping in your bed enjoying the coolness of your bedroom and the comfort of your covers, and people will be contacting you because of who you are!

Your personal brand is not something that you created, rather is what you are continuing to create. Your parents are the initial creators of your personal brand. They determined your name, where you were born, your early schooling, what political affiliation you had, what god you prayed to, and the religion you practiced, if any. They nurtured your structure and influenced how you behaved. As an adult, you can consciously direct your personal brand and change aspects from your childhood that you may no longer agree with or want to be associated with, the same way the natural environment you come from is unlikely to be your current surroundings.

Every single person from your past either has a perceptual belief about you of which could very well no longer be accurate, or has forgotten about you entirely. The latter is a consequence that you're now working to eliminate. Nobody wants to be forgotten as it is against our instinctual behavior and represents a lapse in impact.

You have unknowingly been building your personal brand from the time you had no control over most of the aspects of your life. As a baby, you were contributing to your personal brand. The older you became, the kind of student you were came into play. Were you an easygoing teenager or the problematic class clown? Humorous and radical to think, yet when you break down the implications, you realize that your previous behaviors left impressions on those who once knew you. This alternatively means you have a sense of command over your network as it presently appears. You can reach out to those older acquaintances and associates to ask them to help you build your tomorrow. You may not choose to do so, but the option is there.

Some argue and say the idea of a personal brand is a myth, but let me ask you this, if it were a myth, why is there such a thing as a criminal charge for extreme cases of defamation? Why do public relations firms exist and collectively make billions of dollars every single year preserving the reputations of the corporations and individuals they represent?

Personal branding is very real indeed. The moment you come to understand how to utilize this concept, this idea, and this philosophy, your future will forever change. You will act differently and start to view your reputation with the utmost importance. You will find yourself giving additional thought to what you choose to do, what you say, and with whom you associate. This is not only about keeping an image but concerns developing the understanding that every action in your life has a deserved reaction.

Since the beginning of Neanderthal man, personal branding has existed. The other school of thought claims that personal branding is a new concept and is something that globalization and the expansion of the internet and new technologies have invented. The digitization of *you,* so to speak. Their intentions are pure, but their definitions are misguided and narrow.

It is worth mentioning that the actual term *"personal branding"* is relatively new, coined by the now retired business management consultant, Mr. Tom Peters in his 1997 article *"The Brand Called You"* for FastCompany. The name is contemporary, the *thing* is not. In Napoleon Hill's chapter *"Organized Planning,"* found in *Think and Grow*

Rich, he discusses the idea of developing a portfolio with all of your achievements, successes, and testimonials to land the higher-paying position you privately desire. This is a form of personal branding, as is your résumé, a paper statement of such.

In the next subchapter, *Historical Personal Branding [1.2],* I provide several concrete examples that demonstrate that this is established with precedent. We actually have thousands of years worth of study to learn from and apply. I cannot hope to dive into every possible example, but the examples I do include will be generally recognizable.

Q: How has your perspective on personal branding shifted since reading this subchapter? What has been clarified, compared to your prior understanding on the subject?

1.2 | **Historical Personal Branding**

Are you familiar with the study of anthropology and the movements of ancient man? It is well known that droves of settlers walked the Beringia Land Bridge during an ice age, which at the time connected present day Russia to Alaska. They made their way into North and South America, and established settlements of their own long before being discovered by the rest of the world hundreds of years later. Those very people collectively had personal brands that modern history still discusses, references, and researches. They gave rise to civilizations such as the Mayans and Aztecs. Does the name Montezuma sound familiar?

If we went to the Fertile Crescent and looked at the Mesopotamian people (Babylon), certain kings were more feared than others. King Hammurabi, known for his disciplinarian code, is one such example. Some were revered as fierce and more dominant, their names spreading throughout the East and the West. In Egypt, pharaohs remained in power for hundreds of years and had tens of thousands of people building pyramids and massive tombs in their honor, i.e, Cleopatra, Ramses and Tutankhamun.

How could so few control so many?

Thousands of years later in the north, the Vikings and Norse had kings of their own, some of whom we recognize today. Leif Erickson and the legendary, although somewhat debated figure of Ragnar Lothbrok, are often portrayed as vicious figures in the historical fiction genre and for lacking full historical accuracy, their names are powerful nonetheless.

The rulers of medieval Europe, like Charlemagne and King James, promoted the ideology that they were of divine right to keep their power, whereas they were in essence, normal and just like their fellow countrymen. Blacksmiths, bakers, and the common peasantry looked at them as powerful figures deserving of admiration and reverence. From Alexander the Great who conquered half the world to Genghis Khan who united the Mongols, our history is full of examples of personal branding.

Q: What are some historical examples of people who used their personal brands to achieve a particular goal? What did they do?

1.3 | **The Oldest Form of Branding**

Personal branding, by my estimation, is the world's oldest form of branding. What is the first story in the Christian Theology? *Adam and Eve.* Most religious texts are composed of recounts about people, and if all people have personal brands, that means that we have been studying personal branding all along! I highly doubt you've ever thought about Adam and Eve in this light, but they were the first two people with personal brands. Their sons Cain and Abel, and then the lineage that brought about the tribes of Israel. This is not limited to the Christian body, but to many, if not all of the world's religions.

It's improbable to assume that these people were all consciously thinking to themselves *"What way can I grow my name [or reputation]."* Regardless, their deeds and placement in the historical accounts have left them with legacies lasting thousands and thousands of years. Some figures were driven by the idea of respect, but was Mahatma Gandhi sacrificing himself for vanity or for the greater good?

Many common last names, such as Smith or Baker, were derived from professions. If you were a blacksmith, you would assume the last name of Smith and if you baked bread, you would assume the last name of Baker, which comes from the Old English word *bæcere* which means *"to dry by heat."* The public would know you for this.

As the townsfolk talked, we can imagine that they were making statements along the lines of *"You need to talk to so-and-so baker."* — *"They have the best bread in town."* It is not as if a bakery in the 1500s was referred to as a separate business. The professional's reputation is what drove sales and in this case, is what kept them from starving on the street. Personal branding came first and if it weren't for industrialization, the market would have never allowed for the creation of massive enterprises.

Q: What are your thoughts on personal branding being the oldest form of branding? Do you agree?

1.4 | **New World Examples**

Over the past 150 years, radical communist and totalitarian leaders have risen to power and persuaded the entirety of countries to do their bidding. How could a single man's actions lead to the deaths of millions of people? I am referring to none other than Adolf Hitler. A wretched example, but one that will certainly cause you to stop and think from a critically impartial perspective.

The realization that the person or persons in power all had strong personal brands is evident. They had reputations, fame, and influence. People from all over the developing world knew exactly who they were and it is because of their actions, we study them today. Although the things they are remembered for aren't all honorable and in some cases are awful, we still know of them and their lasting impacts. Fame without influence is like fuel and oxygen without heat. A fire needs all three to burn. Other people are the oxygen, the idea that drives them is the fuel, and the person driving the ideas is the heat.

In the United States of America, the elected officials of the democratic republic represent America, and vicariously all Americans, to other countries. Their actions spark fierce debates amongst citizens, cause other cultures to love or hate us more, and prevent wars out of the fear of retaliation. How these officials get elected, however, is done through leveraging their personal brands. Based on their popularity and how many people side with an individual's *"supposed"* core belief system, emanates a preferred outcome. Given, popularity doesn't always mean they are supported as it's much better to be trusted than to simply be known.

Is it the policy itself that elects the politician or is it the politician who can properly convey the policy? Does the average voter take the time to familiarize themselves with the entire context needed to fully understand that policy, the current nuances, and the reasoning, or would they be more likely to simply vote for the politician because of who they are? I'd make the argument that in many cases personality takes precedence over promises. When there are moments of consequential challenges, policy is going to take priority, but in periods of comfort, it's less about logical thinking and more about emotional ballot-casting.

This extends past that of the United States. Every country has its own system and culture. North Korea may have a dictatorship; the United Kingdom a monarchy with a parliament; and Brazil, a democracy. Despite our cultural or systemic differences, people remain front and center.

Leaders across every profession have understood that by capitalizing on their personal brand, they are attracting opportunities. The more famous they are, the more attention they garner and the more they can do with it. In their minds, there isn't a downside to building their personal brand outside of having their photos taken by the occasional paparazzi and intrusive bloggers looking in on their children and their lives. Hollywood celebrities, charting musicians, well-known artists, models, and prominent CEOs are all using their personal brands and the business of *"them."*

They are not in the business of their profession nearly as much as they are in the business of promotion and building their personal brand. Their endorsements can sway political campaigns, and whatever else they associate themselves with. In terms of investing and equity deals, the entity will automatically perform better than a fledgling startup simply because there is a backing force like an investor, who rather than *(or in addition to)* investing dollars, they're investing attention.

Public figures can be found in the most remote parts of the world. A famous tattoo artist comes to my mind: Whang-od of Buscalan, Philippines. She is over a hundred years old at the time of writing and has single-handedly created a market for tourism for her village. Tourists visit Buscalan just for the chance to see her perform her craft. Not only that, she has preserved and saved the Kalinga style of tattooing from going extinct and was even featured on the cover of one of the most notable fashion magazines in 2023. Remarkable.

When I started consciously building my personal brand in 2017, I used it as a sort of experiment. I was 100% obscure and no one outside my school and classmates knew me. I had no credibility, no social proof, nothing. In a relatively short amount of time I was able to generate awareness around my name and give it power. It is because of my accomplishments, I can without a shadow of a doubt, say that it is possible to go from a nobody to somebody. Sure, it requires work and takes time, but the smallest of efforts will all eventually add up and compound.

This book is written for the individual who wants to see upward mobility accrue with ease. It took me roughly 6 years to see the fruits of my labor payoff.

Over those 72 months, I was busy building relationships, getting quoted in the press, and producing what eventually became high-quality content across various social media platforms. My very first podcast was recorded on an outdated smartphone that was gifted to me by a friend.

As my breakthroughs grew and as my experiences accrued, I invested back into my personal brand and the surrounding technologies, becoming immensely more efficient. Tied with proficiency, what used to take hours, now takes minutes.

Q: What is a *New World Example* of personal branding you'd include?

1.5 | **Fame**

Fame is hard to quantify and perhaps even more difficult to define. The best definition I have come to is: *"Fame is the result of accumulated attention."* Fame is also relative. You could become famous in your industry or famous to everyone. I'll let you decide what definition you choose to use, respective to size, but generally speaking, the more attention you have the more famous you are. There is a term referred to as a *"household name."* A name that is known by virtually every person and is talked about at the dinner table. You could go down the street and knock on your neighbors' doors and nearly all of them will know who they are, could list some of their accomplishments, and might even be a fan, i.e, a *household name*.

Being famous by itself is useless. It is purely a measurement of vanity and the deepest desires of a person's longing for social proof. Outside of feeling good about yourself, what is the purpose of becoming famous? Several years ago, I read a story about an influencer who had an audience of millions on one social media platform. She decided to launch an apparel line *(a common practice to generate revenue)* but to her dismay, she was unable to sell more than four dozen pieces of merchandise. She is an unfortunate perfect example of somebody who had fame and attention but lacked influence. If she was making any sort of impact, she could have easily sold out. Because she lacked any influence over her supposed *"fans,"* she was left with a burdened relationship with her distributor, made a farce in the public's eye, and is now being used as an example of what *not* to do.

Every new relationship contributes to your fame. Whether your content goes viral, you go on a news station, meet someone at an orchestra, or get a contract notarized, these interactions are making additions to your pool of fame.

It is also possible to have fame limited to a niche. When I spoke at the *2024 Atlantic-Oase Professional Conference* in Denver, Colorado, one name kept coming up in my private conversations. This event was specifically for water feature professionals, most of whom were either sellers, distributors, or customers of Atlantic-Oase. For not being in attendance, this gentleman was mentioned by several people and from their stories, appeared to have a dominant personal brand. He is otherwise unknown to anyone outside the water feature industry, but is virtually a household name to those within it.

You could also be famous for the wrong reasons. The crime niche is filled with legions of people who talk about and decipher serial killers and their heinous actions decades after they occurred. Podcasters tell their stories and outlets cover breakthroughs that are made using DNA technology. For having infamy, they aren't influential in the traditional context. Jeffrey Dahmer, Billy the Kid, Jack the Ripper. You know who they are but do they have influence over you? Are you duplicating their crimes? I would hope not.

Fame is impartial to the cause. What you are looking for is influence.

Q: Do you want to be famous? Explain your reasoning. If you do, why is that? If you don't, why not?

1.6 | **Influence**

Influence is represented by trust and the ability to get someone to take action or change the way that they think. Influence is the heat to the fire that is your personal brand. Without it, there is no depth to your reputation. Influence is comparable to the silent frequency of thought—it is not tangible yet it is felt. When an influential person walks into the room, everybody's attention gathers toward them. Influence is established with action and service, and is validated through edification.

Let's take the student who is starting fresh out of high school. They want a career but lack any influence outside of their peer group. They decide to go to college and receive a degree in their respective fields; their hope being that it will lead to the person in charge of company hiring decisions to feel more confident about bringing them on board. If you tack on the validation of the university's reputation and extracurriculars, it results in that bright-eyed student potentially landing the better position. Certain universities have more credibility than others, for instance a graduate from Harvard or Stanford may appear more attractive than the student who graduated from a local community college. Additional certifications and professorial recommendations can also help.

A person who has a negative reputation won't have nearly as much influence as the person who is well regarded. If you are known for being ill-mannered, a scam artist, or have a history of being unreliable, no one will look to you for guidance. Reputation and influence are separate subjects that just so happen to harmonize.

Influence is characterized by creating a sense of confidence and trustworthiness. Someone does not have to fully believe in the thing you're talking about or telling them to do if they trust your intentions or expertise. A doctor may recommend a surgery that you don't see the point in, but decide to move forward with anyway because of their influence over you. The doctor's credibility gives you faith, despite having initial doubts. The abuse of influence is worth noting as the opioid crisis occurred in large part because of the very thing we just discussed.

Biases are a result of influence. Influence itself is impartial, but the aftermath of that influence is not. Being raised in a religious household influences the believer into a way of life. Even racism is manufactured by influence. Somewhere along the way, a person was influenced into a way of thinking that was void of logic. *The byproducts of influence are in large part, emotional.*

The title of this Manifesto includes *"On Fame and Influence"* because of their symbiotic nature. Without influence, fame is useless and without a degree of fame, influence has no reach. This is comparable to the idea of having a strong brand, with a lackluster marketing message. If nobody knows about your brand, how can you expect it to grow? Understanding that influence is the X factor in your personal brand's success, consciously start looking for ways that add to your *"Concentrated Influence."*

Concentrated Influence allows you to direct banked attention towards achieving a particular goal. As you become an influential public figure, you are empowered to direct your influence to sell more copies of your book, land larger features and interviews in the press, sell prospects, get that job you desire, and whatever else you would like to accomplish.

A positive track record vindicates you of third-party concerns and validates your ambitions and capabilities. Influence can also be exploited by those in positions of authority—we will discuss *The*

Dangers of Influence in subchapter [3.8] and under *Destroying Credibility* [5.7].

Q: Who are some of the people who have influence over you? These may be celebrities, mentors, or parents. How did they obtain this influence?

1.7 | **4 Pillar Questions**

Over the years, I have had the honor of working with many professionals, and have regularly emphasized that their personal brand is the way that they can amplify the reach of their faculties and skills. Success requires deliverables after all. Whether it is landing a massive spot within the entertainment industry, or using attention to drive revenue for a business, it's clear that the more people who know who you are, the better.

To guide you as you begin to consciously grow your personal brand, I have included what I refer to as the *4 Pillar Questions*. These are questions I ask my clients to enhance their clarity and understanding.

Question 1: *Why do you want to build your personal brand?*

There must be intention behind building your personal brand. No one does anything without a reason. From my examination, there are three overarching motivations. These reasons are what keeps you moving even when the world comes crashing down and you may be driven by one, a combination of, or all three. Your driving intentions or *forces* may change and that is okay. When significant shifts do occur, reevaluate where you are and identify how you will need to adapt your strategy.

1. **Vanity:** This motive is especially prevalent in the entertainment space and stems from the basic human need to be validated. What better way to be validated than through a successful personal brand, supported by thousands, hundreds of thousands, or millions who know your name? Singers go on stage and are met by stadiums full of people shouting their names and singing their songs. Buildings are named after notable figures; from Carnegie Hall to The Rockefeller Center. After a person's passing what is the point of having buildings named after them if not for vanity?

    God told Adam and Eve not to eat from The Forbidden Tree, but it was because of Eve's vanity that the first bite was taken. I would say vanity is ingrained in our nature. It isn't that you want more attention because of what you can do with it. For those motivated by vanity, *attention itself is the end goal.* I suppose vanity and money go hand in hand, but a famous person when asked may very well choose to remain famous than choose to be rich.

Vanity that is realized, elevates man to the position of a god. Isn't it strange seeing fans become all consumed with gossip? They care more about who a star is sleeping with than their own circumstances. An entire book could be written on this subject alone as it can, at times, serve as a great motivator. Proving others wrong while proving yourself right is one of the most primal feelings. It's when it becomes the only driving force that you start to appear as purely egotistical and as someone who lacks purpose.

2. **Mission:** Successful business people devote their later years and delegate their accumulated resources to causes they care about. Whether their intent is pure I am not here to discuss. A widely known personal brand gives you the overhead to talk about the things you care about, spread awareness, spark and progress movements, and is

conducive to doing good with low cost and high efficiency.

Richard Branson, the magnate behind Virgin brands, is known for his passionate and less-than-corporate stunts early in his career. Subsequently, his successes were followed by public announcements and initiatives in support of climate change, creating a clean environment, and nonprofits dedicated to supporting students. Other examples include Bill Gates and his dedication to eradicating disease, or the public speaker who was a victim of abuse who turned it into their greatest power. These are all examples of the mission-driven archetype.

3. **Money:** The beautiful thing that makes the world go round and round. *Money.* Building your personal brand is a wonderful vehicle for acquiring wealth. Obscurity is the enemy of success and the more attention you have, the more comfortably you can monetize it.

    The young investor that would like to land better deals can use their personal brand to get into rooms with decision makers. It comes in the form of the author or entertainer that feels the need to get on major promotional outlets. The influencer that seeks larger endorsements, the consultant who is able to charge higher rates because of their personal brand, and the lawyer that attracts weighty accounts because their name is mentioned in exclusive circles. Intrapreneurs and employees who position their public image in a positive light to represent their professional qualities will open the door to promotions.

The larger your personal brand becomes, the lower the objection rate falls. You will be told *"no"* less, while the market of opportunity appears to grow. An interesting study could be conducted on the world's most financially affluent. I would dare say that a large sum of them have used their personal brand to accumulate their wealth.

It's not necessary to be famous to generate revenue by way of your personal brand.

I'd like to ask you again, why do you want to build your personal brand? No one is there to judge your motivations.

Question 2: *What do you want to be known for?*

Imagine yourself a few decades from now. What is the foremost thing others know you for? Is there a title you hoped to achieve or an important feat? Is the extent of your reputation limited to your town or state, or are you reaching the nation or world?

It is fair to say you may aspire to be acknowledged for multiple undertakings or fields. What are they? Defining your ambition makes reverse engineering other notable figures who are farther down the path of their careers more straightforward. Question 2.1 is, *What don't you want to be known for?* Consider the opposite to know what to avoid.

Question 3: *Who are you?*

Have you taken any time within the last year to sit down and understand who you are? Possessing an awareness of who you are outside your career is a piece of the puzzle that driven individuals often fail to figure out, although it is the one thing that takes no money or external resources to obtain.

All aspects of your being are components of your personal brand. This includes inimitable characteristics such as the way you look, your body type, your handshake, your interests, your smell, your smile, and your personality. You may be someone who doesn't speak much, but when you do, everyone stops to listen. You may be the talkative one at the office or in your friend group. You may even have the natural ability to make people feel as if they are the only person who matters at a given moment.

No consultant or therapist will ever know you as well as you know yourself. Open up Pandora's Box and put your entire being onto paper. It might not be fun, but understanding all sides to you, good and bad, will serve you well in more ways than one.

Question 4: *How do you get to where you want to be?*

Following the natural order of the previous 3 questions, the Why, What, and Who, we now come to the HOW? It is not wise to receive specific guidance on strategies and steps to help you with your personal brand if you do not take the time to answer the simplest of questions such as: *"What do I want my personal brand to be?"* and *"What benefits do I want to receive because of it?"* The answer to the question *"How do you get there?"* is found throughout this Manifesto.

Every interaction you have is a part of the *how*. If you would like to become a renowned public speaker, crafting a media kit and speaking at your local Chamber of Commerce is a start. If you're aiming to open an art gallery, begin with one stroke of paint. If you want to become an author, writing the first sentence is all it takes to set the groundwork. That is what started my entire writing journey.

Define who you want to be, understand your desired outcomes, and reverse engineer the steps to get there. There is a step-by-step guide at the end of this book but I ask that you don't review it until you finish reading the rest of the chapters first.

1.8 | **Hierarchy of Personal Branding**

To visualize the scale of personal branding, I've created what is called the *Hierarchy of Personal Branding*. This tool is broken down using personal and geographical references but also works by interchanging the words of each level with that of a number range such as 1 to 1,000 or 1,000 to 10,000.

If you think about a person's ambitions for their personal brand, what one may aspire to achieve could be small in the mind of somebody else, while remaining equally huge to another. Earlier I stated that every person should pursue fame, but the truth is not everyone does. Out of those who have this aim, even fewer will find it their reality just like out of the many who pursue wealth, only a handful will ever *"catch"* it.

I would like you to imagine a pyramid with a total of six levels. The majority of people make up the bottom of this pyramid, and as each level ascends, the number dwindles. As it concerns personal branding, we all start at the bottom, which is known as the *Unconscious Incompetent*.

Unconscious Incompetent

This category is a collection of everyone unaware that they have a personal brand. These are the individuals who exist, drifting and living without purposely directing their personal brand. *They do not know what they do not know.* They are unaware that by growing their reputations, their networks, and their publicity, they can benefit from compounded results.

By now, you do not fall into this category as you are aware that your personal brand has an indisputable power, irreplaceable to you, and that it is up to you to harness it. It is because of this category, my work is of the utmost importance as so many could be leading more favorable lives if they simply understood the basics of this field of study.

Friends and Family

For many, when they get good at something, their skill sets will only be known by those that are the closest to them. Think about the mechanic that every family member calls when their car needs repairs. The person who can fix computers or the lively friend that makes everybody belly laugh on game night and could very well be a full-time comedian, but is only known to their friend group.

As we think about the quantity of people this would rarely exceed 100. It's not grandiose nor does it lead to something momentous. *The person is only known by those that they already have a relationship with.* At this stage, they know that they have something that they can build upon, but to take it anywhere else seems far-fetched or too big of a risk.

The Local Hero

Here we have the person who plasters billboards all across the city. The lawyer who is known by people, young and old who run advertisements on afterschool television programs. The realtor who has signs put up in yards all around town. The insurance agent turned politician running for Justice of the Peace. It is the musician who plays local gigs but doesn't get signed to a record label in Los Angeles.

This is *The Local Hero*. They have a degree of respect and trust within a community. We can further break this example down geographically and using an area's census. Whether it's a small town or a big city, the point stands the same. This public awareness requires a degree of exertion and conscious direction. It will not be achieved *unconsciously*.

These individuals must go out of their way to become known by their fellow citizens. They might attend events, shake hands, run ads, aim for school board positions, and so on, as long as they can become known. It is at this place in the *Hierarchy of Personal Branding* that we could replace the title with a number, perhaps 500 or more people will know of the local hero.

The State Representative

As you move up the *Hierarchy of Personal Branding* pyramid, each category requires more effort than the prior one, usually takes more time and more resources, and is generally more difficult to obtain. *The State Representative* is composed of well-established authorities or entertainers, who are known in their region. The United States comprises 50 states, and the person who is known in New York, may not be known in Florida or California. In this category, it is more than reasonable to assume over 100,000 people know about this individual. Although they aren't A-list figures, they have influence over those who care and share something in common.

They can be an "indie success" that sells more than one or two albums and has merchandise. It could be a literal State Representative or a news anchor or radio host that people listen to first thing in the morning and when they get home from work.

Larger opportunities are made available for The State Representative as the person's accomplishments are public.

The National Personality

If you were to go up to anybody off the street in your respective country and ask them *"Who is this person?"* while holding up a picture of a notable figure, they would be able to answer you. *The National Personality* is full of artists, celebrities, corporate executives, experienced leaders, national news anchors, and politicians. Out of every 100,000, maybe 1 is on this level. As you go up the pyramid, the degree of influence does in parallel. These individuals have massive degrees of exposure, are represented by agents, have ghostwriters and big-wig editors, and teams of professionals dedicated to that one person's achievements.

They can hardly walk in public without being recognized. The impact a person has at this level cannot be understated as their smallest words may get picked up and discussed in tabloids and outlets.

The International Icon

By putting yourself into the public's view, you are positioned in such a way that often one-sided relationships begin to develop. You will potentially have millions of people who know and trust you, but you may not know they exist. International Icons have such fame and influence that they can change the outcome of wars, elections, and in some cases the economy. The niche of an Icon is irrelevant as long as they have global awareness.

This is the world-touring artist that generates billions of dollars in tourism revenue for the city they play in. It is the public billionaire that posts memes for fun or the presidents of nations. These individuals use a wide range of marketing channels to get their message out to the masses and curate rapport at scale.

Rapport is trust and a person's connection with another human. It begins growing or being destroyed the moment a stranger comes in contact with you. When rapport is built, what started as a follower relationship is transmuted into a fan, and then into a loyal supporter. People like feeling that they are a part of something bigger and since celebrities portray the image of an extraordinary life that is out of reach for the normal person, they attract waves of incoming support. Isolated ecosystems form amongst their fans which to outsiders may come across as cult-like. *International Icons* make up less than .01% of the population.

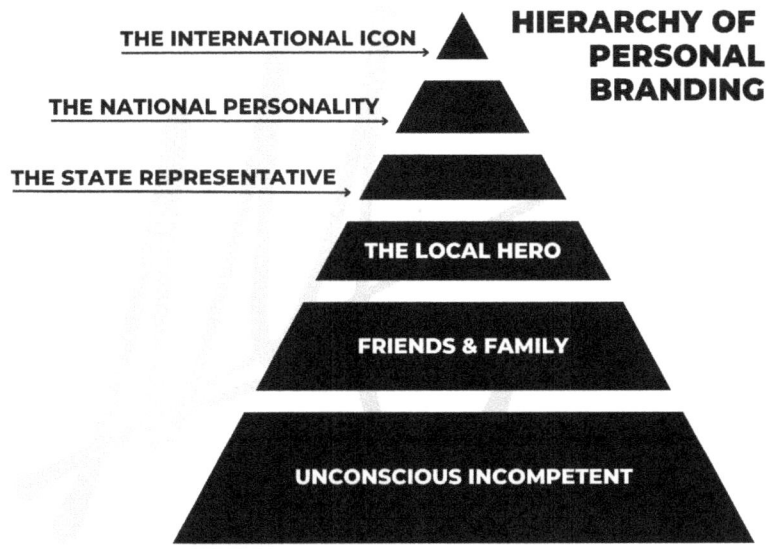

Q: What are examples from your own life of people who fall under the *Hierarchy of Personal Branding?* What level do you want to reach yourself?

| 2 |

The 4 Laws of Personal Branding

A proclamation of depth, progression, and scale

2.1 | The Law of Familiarity

"As a person becomes more familiar with a subject through the use of their 5 senses, the more they naturally come to trust it."

As you perpetually see something for the first time, whether it is a piece of information, a person, or a place, you have a sense of wonder and amazement for it. Your curiosity is bolstered, and you might be excited to learn more or on the contrary, uncertain and apprehensive.

When you move to a city, you'll be enamored by all of the houses and new sights, but within a year, the mountains in the background become familiar. It's not that you don't think it's any less great, rather, you are used to the experience. The dimly lit streets that you felt estranged from, you now drive out of habit. You have your favorite restaurants, shop at your preferred grocery stores, and have seen the same animals at the zoo with your children. This is identical to people.

Do you remember the beginning of the school year? The feelings you felt as summer came to a close and you got your upcoming schedule? At orientation you visited your classes, met your teachers, and received an exhaustive list of supplies. There may have initially been some anxiety and nervousness built up because you were not familiar with the new environment you were about to enter into. It likely took you a couple of weeks or longer to get comfortable and your classmates probably shared similar experiences. They weren't certain about you. They didn't know if you would be their friend, their bully, or the kid that they could cheat off during a test, or the kid who would try to cheat off of them.

By the end of the school year, you knew everybody. *It wasn't so distant.* This is caused by the *Law of Familiarity*. The more you get accustomed to something, the fewer questions exist around it. In the same way, as you communicate your personal brand's message and showcase your being, people will become familiar with you from afar.

Celebrities do not know all of their fans, but their fans know their life story, their career, their interests, where they were born, their spouses, and so many more details that would be considered obsessive.

You don't have to be an *International Icon [1.8]*, but through the use of advertising and media channels you can become that authority and well-known figure so that when somebody does want to connect with you, buy from you, or support you, they are already familiar with your work and what you stand for. This is the Law of Familiarity.

Rapport is built by repeated contact and points of similarity. This leads to the second Law, the *Law of Connection.*

Q: How have you seen the Law of Familiarity in your own life?

2.2 | **The Law of Connection**

"People look for similarities and points of relatability. The more you can emotionally connect with an individual, the deeper their resonance."

After the chapter *Personal Skills [7]*, I have included my paper *Identity Positioning: A Macroscopic View on Personal Branding.* In it, I highlight the importance of showing your personal side and present my proprietary strategy of the same name. You will find a more comprehensive breakdown of how *the Law of Connection* ties together with the *Law of Familiarity [2.1]*.

The Law of Connection gives others a reason to care. After all, *personal* is the first part of a *personal brand.* You would not marry a person who does not share anything in common with you. You would not be loyal to a contractor if you didn't build a relationship with them. You would not vote for a politician who you can't relate with, at least to some degree. Think about those closest to you. Are they close because of what they can get from you, or because they like you? Perhaps a favorite hobby is shared, a genre of music, a past trauma even. The time spent together nurtures that bond and as you are building your personal brand, find ways to connect and make someone feel as if they have known you for years. Ask questions about their lives, family, and future. See what you have in common, or don't for that matter. *Transparency leads to trust.*

Our culture as it exists today is filled with false promises, controlled narratives, and *fluff*. Having the situational awareness of when to share stories or reflect on hard lessons learned shows that you are a real person that isn't trying to as they say "*Fake it till they make it.*"

Connection leads to security. We have no issue with leaving strangers, but rarely do we want to leave our friends. Use your personal brand to make friends at scale!

Q: Who is somebody that started as a stranger to you, but is now a close friend or mentor? What led to this relationship's growth?

2.3 | **The Law of Fame and Influence**

"Fame and Influence have a symbiotic relationship and when combined, result in the most ideal outcome for personal brands. Alone, their impacts are diminished."

Fame is developed through mass market appeal, marketing channels, and discussions by third parties. Fame itself holds no power unless combined with influence. Many people who possess influence are also naturally famous, but not all people who have fame are influential. Remember that *influence is the ability to get a person or group of persons to do or believe something by your words alone.*

    The Law of Fame and Influence is a representation of potential. Fame by itself is empty vanity and influence alone is limited in exposure. When a quantifiable measurement of fame is expressed with the emotional aspects of influence, whatever you seek to achieve will be expedited.

    It is also a numbers game. If you have a community of thousands, there will assuredly be a difference to the degree of influence you have from person-to-person. Some may follow you more closely and take everything you say to heart, whereas others only observe you from a distance. Your influence should resonate deep enough with those close observers that it compensates for those who are less engaged.

Q: Who is a famous person who holds equal influence? What makes them influential as opposed to just being famous?

2.4 | **The Law of Personal Branding**

"A personal brand can only be created with the introduction of new life. A personal brand cannot be destroyed, regardless of the death of the person it belongs to. A personal brand can, however, be forgotten."

The Law of Personal Branding infers that a personal brand is an intangible creation that occurs the moment a person is conceived in the mind of a parent and is realized at birth. A personal brand will always exist, regardless of the lack of records or remembrance. A personal brand is the unique fingerprint of every human who has ever lived. Whatever part a person plays during their life has an eternal contribution to the universe. A personal brand is not something that can be avoided or destroyed in the literal sense.

For something intangible, it tangibly may be directed, grown, and scaled. Being fully forgotten or running out of relevance is the closest you can get to *destroying* a personal brand. This Law puts relativity into perspective. If put on the spot, could you recall the name of your great-great grandparent? It would be impressive if you could, but for the average person, after the first *great*, it goes dark.

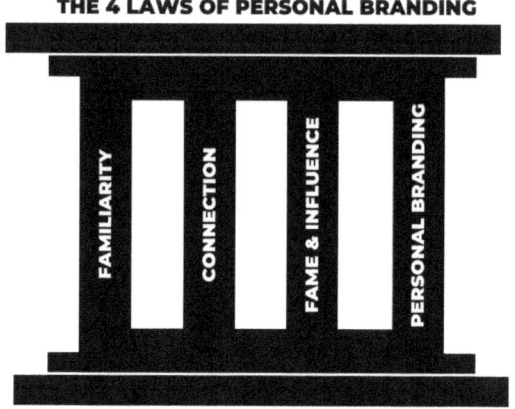

These 4 Laws make up not only the foundation of your personal brand but of our society and how we interact with those around us. Their significance can't be understated as without The Law of Familiarity, The Law of Connection doesn't exist. Without The Law of Fame and Influence, The Law of Personal Branding loses impact and without The Law of Personal Branding, it all collapses.

T: Do some research into your lineage and find a distant grandparent more than 3 generations back. Learn about their life if possible.

| 3 |

Mindset

The intrapersonal ways of thinking and living required to develop a successful personal brand

3.1 | **Becoming The 1%**

When you hear the term 1% what is the first thought that comes to your mind? Chances are if you are like most, you think about money. A financial metric; people who have reached a particular point of monetary status. Depending on the country, the state, or the local you live in, the technical 1% can vary, but this is not the topic I'm here to cover.

The concept of the 1% extends much farther than finances. It extends to an overall way of being. There is a quote that says *"How you do one thing is how you do anything."* Anyone who believes they can pursue the 1% in one area of life, without pursuing the 1% in another is a fool.

In all aspects of life, there will be the top 1%. The select few who outperform the rest time and time again, have payoffs that supersede wildest beliefs and are largely fulfilled in their day-to-day lives. This is regarding business, faith, finances, health, lifestyle, relationships, and even intrapersonal conversations.

The marketplace is not looking for another person to mindlessly subscribe to. *The marketplace is looking for the anomaly.* By deliberately choosing to be in the category of the 1% you are making it easier for people to latch on and live through you by proxy. *The 99% are looking for the 1% to follow.* Be aware as this treads a very thin line between pure ego and strategy.

It is the conversation around the Creator versus the Consumer. There is no shortage of consumerism, but we are driven by advancement. With your growth and achievements, you will become more appealing and in turn the label of *"public figure"* becomes justifiable.

Embodying the public persona you set forth will serve you in more ways than one. If you're performing at or above your expectations, is doubt more or less likely to creep in? If you're showing up in a timely manner and continuing to hit new heights, will the internal voice that propagates imposter syndrome have as much sway? No.

When John F. Kennedy asked Dr. Wernher von Braun what it would take to get man to the moon, he replied with: *"The will to do so."* Once the decision was made, the determination set, they sought out the necessary equations and research to send that rocket to space and ultimately land on what is little more than a big rock attached to our Earth's orbit. It wasn't just the research itself, but also the people behind the research which improved. Information alone doesn't have any power, it is when that information is applied, its power is expressed.

Self improvement must play a pivotal role in your life. Your obsession with growth must get to a point where the times that you are not growing make you feel off; that those moments are not how it should be. This is your subconscious mind reaffirming the standard you have set. In this day and age, with all of our technology and access to resources like artificial intelligence, there is little excuse as to why you are not actively seeking out ways to become more advanced.

Becoming the 1% marks the time for you to step into a role of leadership. Never take advice from somebody who doesn't have the experience in an area of life that you want to have for yourself. Be selective of the mentors or public figures you look to for advice as you will never have all of the energy in the world to follow every person you might want to.

Your personal brand in large part is like a lighthouse to a boat on a stormy night. The boat, which is your community, is looking to you for some feeling or guidance. You want to be the person who entertains them, educates them, motivates/inspires them, and connects with them on personal levels. You are the center of attention but unlike the mindless person that does not deserve it, you have something to offer.

This could be reflected in your content, the books you write, the speeches you deliver, and the words of encouragement you offer when having coffee with a friend going through a rough time.

Q: Why would someone choose to follow another person? Think about what makes them appealing.

3.2 | Intensity and Aggressive Patience

Aggressive Patience is the understanding that your goals and vision take time to achieve. No matter the frame of time, it mustn't prevent you from taking action steps that bring you closer to your objectives.

Patience alone becomes an excuse for your lack of execution whereas aggressiveness alone leads to a blatant disregard for relationships, details that matter, and potential impacts to one's reputation. When combined, great things are the result. Take the story of *The Hare & The Tortoise* by the ancient Greek storyteller Aesop. We all know it and who comes out as the winner of the race? The Tortoise. Albeit, move faster than one of nature's slowest animals, adopt the tenacity of the Tortoise, and do not stop pushing your personal brand, unlike the rabbit that stops to take a nap under a tree. There are many beliefs on how success is achieved but what I know as fact, is those who implement their ideas will see things come to fruition far faster than those that overthink without implementing.

Overthinking leads to a lack of effort altogether; rumination is something I struggled with at length, and it makes the smallest tasks appear to be insurmountable. You must come to appreciate your mind's search for answers yet I implore you to not get caught in the trap of questioning what you will do next for too long. This extends well outside of the conversation of personal branding.

Aggressive Patience tied with a reasonable degree of compulsiveness is how you eliminate some of these circumstances and make headway others are too fearful to. Compulsiveness can serve you well but I am not encouraging you to behave so compulsively that you lack strategy or burn out. If you can take a firm strategy, either by hiring a personal brand consultant or coming up with your own, you will have a step-by-step guide you can follow with intense action.

Let's say your network has run dry and your list of prospects and people who are engaging with you isn't what it used to be. If you have already built a network once before, you likely know exactly what you need to do to build it again. Not only can you prevent it from running dry in the future, you also understand what you did or did not do, and are capable of applying the same course of action that worked. Instead of taking you five years to connect with a thousand people, you can implement *The*

Power of 3 [6.5] and connect with brand-new faces on a daily basis.

For one final exercise in this subchapter, I'd like for you to stand up and stay in place for an hour. Don't move and don't take a step forward; do nothing and be still! Obviously, you're not about to do this but this is a representation of what happens when you fall victim to *Analysis Paralysis*. This is a condition caused by the lack of clarity and the obsession over details. Not being clear or perfect and still making progress is more beneficial than taking forever to come up with the best hypothetical plan.

There are hundreds of strategies you can use for your personal brand, thousands of potential outcomes, and eventually millions of moving parts. You will never master or implement all of them. Your task is not to be a data scientist who analyzes every data point; it is to be an executor who gets things done. If it means temporarily going back to the basics to establish momentum, so be it. *Momentum is the precursor to rapid growth.*

T: What are you going to do to develop your aggressive patience and proper intensity?

3.3 | **Longevity**

When looking to build a grounded personal brand, regardless of what level of the *Hierarchy of Personal Branding [1.8]* you want to find yourself at, aligning your mindset with your vision is a requirement. This is your validation to go all in and treat your personal brand as if it were a business.

Your personal brand has a following, an image, a reputation, and service/s, and must be appreciated as a lifelong commitment.

A project that requires consistent effort.

A hobby that is never truly mastered.

There is no highest degree with your personal brand.

You do not have to be a student of theology to value religion. Many religions have been based around a primary character with a remarkable and one-of-a-kind personal brand. Think about Jesus Christ and Christianity, the Prophet Muhammad and Islam, or Siddhartha Gautama and Buddhism. There are direct ties between the worship of a divine power and that of an individual who presented a new line of thinking to the public.

Do you suppose any of these religions or pathways to living would have the devotees they do today if it were not for an undeniable tenacity to spread their beliefs? *I think not.* The level of zealousness of these religious leaders led to their systems of belief being adopted in some cases, by billions of people and worshipped for millennia.

A personal quote I strive to live by is *"At the center of all achievement is personal growth."* Others have already made mistakes before we were ever dreamt of. We can learn from the actions of others and examine their findings without having to take the detrimental or painful hits for ourselves. This is the closest we can come to taking a shortcut to success. *Personal development is the way we cut time frames.*

Reading this Manifesto is a form of personal development. Do what you are doing right now to a degree that you have never done before as the more information you absorb and then apply, the better off you'll be. I've never heard of somebody who learned too much, although I have witnessed many who absorbed too little. Your personal brand is a lifelong commitment and to think that you can hit it big with one swing is half-witted. No intention compensates for a lack of execution.

Longevity is about creating a strong foundation followed by preserving the structure. The oldest paintings are kept safe by trained conservators and although It may take a decade for momentum to pick up, it was built off of a series of seeds you planted and then nurtured. All of the articles you wrote, interactions you had, interviews you showed up to, and pieces of content you created are stacked onto one another.

Q: How did the aforementioned figures build longevity with their personal brands? Why did their names not just die out?

3.4 | **Perspective and Doubt**

How do we navigate the negative words and doubts coming from the people around us? Anyone who starts a business gets told all of the risks and reasons it might not work. In a similar fashion, the moment you decide to consciously build your personal brand, you are setting yourself up to be a target for people who doubt.

If the people closest to you do not view you as an authority, or somebody worthy of as they say, *grandiosity,* it should not come as a surprise. In their mind, they still see you as the kid they grew up with, or as their son or daughter.

There is no use trying to convince anybody. Let your actions and personal brand do the speaking. How can you expect others to support you when up until this point you haven't given them any reason to? A brand-new product has to be validated by the marketplace as does your personal brand. Your results can help motivate you and remind you of who you are and what you are capable of. Doubt is normal, but staying complacent should not be a symptom. Those who achieve great success carry themselves in such a way that impresses confidence on others. The quiet, or even unconfident person is not going to be the public speaker or have millions of people looking to them for guidance. To use the example of Gandhi once again, he was able to change a nation without lifting a finger but operated with confidence and was zealous in his mission.

Boldness of character is needed to take calculated risks. Making a game out of it helps me find more joy—After all, what is the worst that can happen? Recording a video for the first time may appear like you're climbing Mount Kilimanjaro. I implore you to get in front of the camera and speak. Will you be great at it on your first try? Probably not but by the thousandth video, your skill set will match what was once *blind confidence* and belief. When I first started in business, I operated out of a youthful arrogance. There was cockiness in my character and voice as I was trying to convince other people and frankly, I was trying to convince myself. Something remarkable eventually happened as I began to understand the world in a more mature sense and the things that worked and the things that didn't. Cockiness evolved into confidence. From that point on, I adopted the tenacity I had in my youth and applied it to the confidence in knowing I was able to achieve a specific result. In turn, everything was amplified.

A first-time startup founder may launch a product that they know is not 100% complete, but may still have meteoric adoption. Eventually, they improve their products and their offer, they listen to feedback, and they develop something great. As you invest in yourself, through audiobooks, courses or programs, coaching, podcasts, and reading you're effectively adding more figurative *"features."* Your personal growth will allow you to speak in a more warranted manner resulting in an air of influence.

I am personally motivated by a sort of dark energy. I understand this might not appeal to some, but if you can take that chip on your shoulder and carry that weight, you can prove anybody who doubted you wrong. This is not about going back to them in a couple of years to say *"I told you so."* Its purpose is to live inside of you, for you to examine and be fueled by, and to know that you accomplished and are accomplishing something significant despite being told you couldn't. People who are doing better than you will never talk down on you. It is only the people who are looking up who wish to bring people down.

Q: How has your confidence grown from when you first started in your business or profession?

3.5 | **Keeping the Right Attitude**

I have never been somebody who wakes up in a high-vibration state of mind. It takes me time to get out of bed and a few cups of coffee before I feel ready to take on the world. You can expect your attitude and degree of optimism to fluctuate. Building your personal brand is an added responsibility that you take on and some days your post may not perform as well as you would like, you may get rejected whilst pitching yourself to a publication, or somebody will talk down to you.

Keeping the right attitude is not easy although with practice, you will develop the self-awareness of how you are feeling. If a thought creeps into your mind such as *"Why am I doing this,"* or *"Is this really worth it,"* put a stop to it right then and there. Say firmly to yourself *"Absolutely not"* and snap your fingers to change your emotional state.

Find some sort of spiritual practice that aligns you back to the center. Take time to meditate, go for a walk, or have lunch with a friend. Maintaining an attitude of optimism as a leader is of the utmost importance because the public is not looking for Debbie Downers to support. If you are a public pessimist, you might as well be like everybody else.

If you speak without self-assurance, you lack credence.

Excellence is your obligation. Is it possible to truly be confident if your performance is below your expectations? There are no downsides to excellence. Setting a standard for yourself will only lead to better outcomes, and in fairness it is not proper to expect others to follow you on your journey if your execution is subpar. Make it a habit to go the extra mile. Send that message, respond to the comment, clean up after yourself in the gym, pick up the piece of trash in the road, and return the shopping cart. *False idols are cast aside.*

This is a call to action for honesty. Although your motivating factor for building your personal brand might be vanity, your mindset should not be vain. Impartiality is the ability to take a step back and evaluate your performance, results, and lack thereof. It's your ability to look for weaknesses in your strategy and intrinsic behaviors. It will be uncomfortable, and yet it is a necessary element for your progression. If you find yourself falling short of your obligation to excellence, correct yourself as soon as you can. The longer you wait to make a change the more likely what you want to change becomes a bad habit and a misguided system of thought. Being impartial isn't about beating yourself up, it's about optimization.

If you're connected with somebody whose content has been excelling, see what advice they would have for you. If your performance in life and with your personal brand is still slacking, cast your ego aside, and ask yourself why. What are you doing that you shouldn't be doing, and what could you be doing that you're not? What are you doing a little that you need to do more? Impartiality is a representation of maturity.

As I'll cover in the chapter on *Giving Endorsements [5.11],* being impartial is also what you will be using to draw proper logical conclusions rather than relying solely on your emotions. It's thinking with your head, not your heart. Business owners and executives have to be impartial and look at the facts when they're making difficult decisions, such as hiring or firing somebody and large transactions. Should you hire somebody just because you were friends with them? Probably not.

Being partial to yourself, your actions, your personal brand, the people you support and all other things considered, are all rooted in emotions, but in order for you to find ways of improvement or better outcomes it's up to you to operate on a higher frequency. Deal with facts instead of theory and strategy instead of convenience.

The same can be said about dealing with your ambitions. If you set the goal of becoming the Number 1 expert in your field, is that the best goal you can set? You can become a top expert in time, but if you're just starting, you have to balance strategic thinking with your ego drive.

Visualize you are alone in a room sitting at a desk. The air is cool, comfortable, and without windows—It almost resembles an interrogation room. Now go outside of your body so that you're sitting across the table and making eye contact with yourself. With honesty and the sole intent of progress, examine your past and current actions, evaluate outcomes, and be open in terms of your health and appearance. Be impartial and be your biggest critic. Write everything down on paper and start executing. You can also confide in those who have the best intentions for you such as associates, bosses, close friends, and anyone else you believe wouldn't be too soft in their feedback. Ask them for an honest peer-performance review.

If you've gained weight, take control of your health. If you've slacked off on marketing, start putting yourself out there. If your expertise has fallen behind, freshen up on your skills. Being fueled by pride will cause you to lie to the one person you should never lie to.

Q: What is an example when you let your attitude falter? How did it affect your results?

3.6 | **Burnout and Competition**

"I give up." — These are three words that should never come out of your mouth. *Burnout* is marked by a period of inaction. It is a time where questions creep in and focus is lost; it is manifested as doubt grows. A wildfire cannot grow without oxygen so suffocate those doubts before they spread.

The simple solution to burnout is more execution. Your personal brand is not growing as much as you would like? *So what?* Sure, you got told no, or you didn't hear back from a pitch. *So what?* Is that the reason that you give up? Apply more pressure and maintain momentum. Are you more likely to doubt yourself when things are going great or are you more likely to doubt yourself when things aren't going your way?

Become such an immovable force that it would nearly impossible to stop you. Do not sit in pity or self loathing, instead embrace it as dark energy and again, carry that weight.

If you're not willing to do this, close this book and forget you ever picked it up. Realistically speaking, it will take you at least 3 years to really submit to your personal brand and 5 for everything to accelerate. The first 36 months is a period of trial and error. Around month 60, you'll get good and focused. By the time you cross the decade mark, you should have everything down to a science and enough credibility where if you decided to take a temporary break, you can pick it back up where you left it. *Letting burnout dictate you is weak.*

Despite all of the clichés and what feel-good *"motivators"* tell you, competition is very real. Regardless of what business you're building, what career path you're pursuing, or what you want your personal brand to be known for, you will be competing with an innumerable amount of people. From the 4+ billion people who are on the internet, many whom are creating content, to the local professional who is also out there networking. It is difficult to stand out and gain that attention when everybody else is fighting for it.

The beautiful thing about building your personal brand is it is a way for you to cut through all of the noise. If you are not positioned as a public figure, *as a top person worth following,* you will get lost in all of this chatter. Your personal brand must be established in such a way that demands respect and commands influence. You should dominate your competition. Crafting such a strong personal brand that it is impossible for another person to doubt you or to question your authority and credibility. What you have accomplished and what you have brought and contributed to the marketplace are weapons in your arsenal.

I have gamified my process and I am constantly looking for ways that I can stand above the rest. This can be in gaining quotes in authoritative press articles, writing contributor pieces for publications and leveraging their platform's credibility, to producing content that is constantly improving in editing style and flow.

Find others who are building their personal brands in a similar field or niche to use as measurements in reference to where you want to be. There are going people who have been doing it longer and have accomplishments to back it up. It is not about ruining their life as it is about wanting to get to their level and supersede them. A track record that you can reverse engineer and apply. Competition is a blessing, as without it, the market would not evolve.

We can see this in capitalism and free enterprise where companies that compete with one another lead to breakthroughs in innovation. Mankind made so many leaps forward during the Cold War because the United States was competing with Soviet Russia. To use a previous example, the United States was competing with other countries to have the first man step foot on the moon. These are the times where character is built.

If you are not a competitive person, you are losing out on a tremendous amount of potential. You are at a massive disadvantage and are not capable of serving all of the people that you could lead or otherwise impact. Your obligation is not only excellence, your obligation is to get people to know about you because you have the ability to help them. It becomes less about competing with another person and more about competing with yourself.

This is a mental game that you can start playing in times where morale is low. *You versus You*. Those periods of doubts and imposter syndrome can fuel your fire by introducing an enemy. Your current version is fighting with the person you are working to become. If you're losing weight you're not competing with other people to get into better shape, you're competing with yourself. To get the most out of your time, competing with yourself as well as competing with another individual will push you all the more and in like, increase your efforts. The world is not some utopia, so leave the idea that competition does not exist in the past.

Even the most gifted person must work to develop and nurture their talents. You could be blessed with height, but that does not mean you would make a good basketball player. Drawing may come easy to you, but you can still benefit from learning new techniques, understanding Color Theory and honing your craft. Your speaking voice may be authoritative, yet you occasionally stutter. The idea that talent alone is what makes a person successful is fallacious. It is not a necessity to have talent. It is a necessity to have *willpower*.

Willpower is the force you call upon that allows you to push through and accomplish tasks even if you do not physically feel like it. You could be emotionally drained, mentally tired, physically exhausted, but you understand that in order to achieve your intended outcomes, things still need to get done. Willpower is expressed in getting up early and forcing yourself out of bed, going the extra mile on a client meeting, and taking the phone call when you don't *"feel like it."* One does not become the top 1% in their profession without willpower and mental discipline. Will is a sword in need of frequent sharpening.

Compile your wins. Every time that you make a decision that goes against the weak voice inside of your head, latch on to that feeling and tell yourself that you did something good. Despite every fiber of your being telling you to be lazy, you powered through, executed willpower, and remained disciplined. This puts you above the average person.

In time, you will develop yourself into a sharp individual with full self control. I believe it is paramount to mention willpower in a book about personal branding, as every person that you look up to has made the conscious decision to take on more responsibility.

There is a hierarchy to accomplishments. It is not like a magic wand was waved when certain people became endowed with success. They chose success and strived towards it.

Q: Have you ever experienced burnout? How did you get out of it?

3.7 | **The Dangers of Fame**

Fame in and of itself is not a risk as it is impartial and lacks possessive power. Yes, there is the possibility of tenacious paparazzis or stalkers when fame is broadened, but what you do with that fame is worth addressing. Several years ago I was approached by a business owner, if you can even call him that. He ran an affiliate business model and botted social media accounts. On our first call he shared a childish hypothetical situation. Essentially, he used the example that if you went to the bar and wanted to take home a woman, would she be more attracted to the person who had 2,000 followers or 100,000?

Forget the legitimacy of the following, it was all about appearances. A perfect representation of misdirected vanity and fabricated fame. Fame is both a burden and a blessing. Why would someone be more likely to choose the individual with more followers? Validation.

When I was flown out in 2019 to Vidcon by Facebook as one of their Star Creators, I saw first hand the deep need for validation. I remember one artist throwing money into the crowd around him, fans lining up at booths to take photos with their favorite influencers, and the constant need to create. It was a continuous cycle of validation by association. I believe fame can be used to open up doors that are closed to the general public, but step over too much, Lust, Greed, and Envy will ensue. They are regarded as deadly sins with good reason.

Losing sight of the bigger picture and the intent behind building your personal brand is what leads to the path of depravity and poor decision making. In the subchapter *Destroying Credibility [5.7]* I included multiple unnamed examples where Icons who were at one time well regarded, used their fame opportunistically and lost it all.

Q: Think about someone in culture who accumulated a lot of fame and either lost it, or went down a dark path. How did it happen and what could they have done to prevent it?

3.8 | **The Dangers of Influence**

Wielding influence is by far more dangerous than having fame. Influence is concentrated power. At the beginning, I asked the question, *"What if you could get nations to do your bidding?"* I can think of no better example of the dark side of influence than Adolf Hitler. One man, through powerful speeches and strategic control of the media, was able to twist a sense of nationalism, prompting a country that felt obligated to war and rallied against an entire group of people. He used his political office to inflict pain, charisma to grow his influence, and snubbed out the opposition giving him uncontested rule.

The same can be said in Karl Marx's ideology of Marxism, or Mao Zedong in China. These are three men who had profound impacts on billions of people, whose actions led to the deaths of millions. Influence in the symbolic hands of dark triad types, when unchallenged or outmaneuvered, has consequences that are impossible to understate.

As you are growing your own influence, my hope is that you do good with it. Influence is both a gift and honor deserving of respect. You have an obligation to adhere to the ethics of man. Take the salesman who is extremely skilled at selling. Just because they can sell someone something, does not mean that they should. Be cautious with your endorsements, research things before you speak, and understand your ideologies are no longer your own.

Making a quick joke to your audience may be taken seriously and a statement pulled out of context could present you in an erroneous light. The chapter on *Reputation Management [5]* covers examples such as these.

There is a psychological phenomenon known as *The Halo Effect* which is a form of cognitive bias people have towards a specific individual or thing based on a singular trait. We assume a person is somehow greater than we are based on a variety of factors such as previous accolades, influence, social circles, and wealth. It is because of this, celebrities exist. The smallest piece of information can have a far reaching impact on perceptions. Inversely, a second phenomenon known as *The Horn Effect* may lead to reaching ramifications.

Albeit less known than the Halo Effect, the Horn Effect is when somebody bases their entire perception of a person or thing off of one aspect which in their mind they deem negative. Let's say you knew somebody who was bald and it just so happens that you greatly disliked them. Maybe their personality was off-putting, you just couldn't see eye-to-eye, or they treated you poorly. The Horn Effect bias causes your subconscious mind to create emotions upon meeting somebody else who also happens to be bald. You may find yourself drawing similar conclusions about them, with no further evidence aside from the association with their lack of hair. It sounds ridiculous but this also applies to your personal brand and how you manage your reputation.

The Horn Effect results in misguided assumptions by association with negative past memories, therefore producing negative repercussions. Things that you might not even think about such as smoking a cigar, drinking liquor in public, and wearing pajamas to go to the grocery store all influence how another person perceives you and will produce lasting impressions that you will continuously have to work to change if you wish to improve your reputation in their minds.

T: Spend the next few minutes researching some of the most influential people throughout history. What shared experiences or traits did they possess?

| 4 |

Branding

How to develop the public expression of your internal ambitions

4.1 | **Who Are You?**

As you read this, I want you to think about some of your recent interactions. If you were to go up to somebody and ask them how they are doing, most of the time they will respond by referencing their work or career. Maybe their job is overworking them, they feel underpaid, and they're stressed out. There's so much emphasis on the professional side, they miss out on one of the most important parts of their identity. The phrase *"personal brand"* is two-sided, it has two words. On the left, you have the word *personal* which consists of aspects of your personal caricature such as your faith, hobbies, interests, passions, political beliefs, and your personality; all of the novelties that your friends love or hate about you.

On the right side you have *"brand"* which represents your professional life and career. Brand describes the things that make you money, your credibility, your expertise, and the challenges you have overcome to get to where you are at. Your identity and your personal brand is more than just your career. Showcasing your personal side is a way to build *Rapport*, the subject of which we will discuss in subchapter *[4.4]*. Every person I have used as an example in this book has a personal brand. I want you to especially focus on the second word *"brand."* What is branding versus marketing?

Let's define them as: *branding is what people know you as*, whereas marketing is *how you get more people to know about you.*

There are often conversations in professional communities regarding the complexity and importance of branding in relation to marketing. Some believe that branding is superior to marketing and others believe that marketing is essential to branding's success. Instead of viewing the two as greater or less than one another, it is best to view them as equals. As two sides of the same coin, two tools that can only properly function when the other is present.

If your brand is strong with succinct messaging and effective designs but lacks in marketing, you'd only have your family, friends, and neighbors know who you are or about what you do. Anything past these social circles, you'd be unknown.

If your marketing is on point, but your brand is lacking, what ends up happening is a massive influx of attention accompanied by a very low rate of conversion. This applies to both digital and physical spectrums.

Once you apply a strong brand with a strong marketing strategy, you achieve a synergistic energy that allows you to become a powerhouse in any area you direct focus towards. By positioning yourself as a thought leader or as a person of public interest, and through the application of as many forms of marketing as possible, your conversions will be increased and you will have fewer people questioning your credibility. To have somebody question who you are and why they should care about what you do is a horrible situation to be in. This form of diminishment hurts the ego and can lead to things like imposter syndrome and low self belief.

Who you are also applies to the titles you've earned. For example, with the publication of the First Edition of this book, I was able to use the title of author. When you launch a podcast, you're a podcast host. From the moment you launch a business, you're a business owner. If you went to school for law and become a lawyer, you are a lawyer. Doctors have PhDs and even after completing years of intensive schooling and training, medical students must successfully finish their thesis to earn the right to be referred to as Dr. *(their name)*.

Titles, regardless of the length of time that you've held them, contribute to your credibility. Our entire civilization operates on titles that convey trust. Using them to your advantage makes it easier for people to understand who you are and what you are about, simultaneously assisting you in making introductions. Imagine you're going on for an interview and they say *"Today we are interviewing a renowned author, podcast host, business owner, and serial entrepreneur."* Compared to *"Today we have XYZ on the show."* These little tidbits of information make it easier to convey and prove relevance to the subject matter and the target market.

In large part, titles are vanity metrics, which feel good to say and have next to your name, but it is more so about what they can do for you versus how they make you feel. It's up to you to determine how many titles you associate with your personal brand.

If you have done 25 different things, you might not want to include all 25 in your introductions and materials. Pick the ones that are the most relevant to what you want to be known for. The most impactful titles will be the ones people remember and associate with you. If you once launched a podcast in 2008 and have not had one since, does it make sense for you to say that you're a podcast host?

Q: What are standout interests or traits about you that can be used as a personal hook?

4.2 | **What Makes Your Personal Brand**

We've already distinguished that your personal brand is *you, t*here's no question about it, but what makes you, you? There are 5 main factors we'll be discussing in this subchapter: *Characteristics, Faith, Personal Beliefs, Profession,* and *Hobbies*. They are all reflections of each other and are tied closely together. Your faith determines many of your beliefs, and your beliefs influence your characteristics. Based on your profession, you may behave differently than some others. Understanding these targeted aspects of your behavior and composition gives you a competitive advantage in terms of promotion and positioning yourself amongst your peers.

1. **Characteristics:** Both intrinsic and extrinsic. Intrinsic relates to your personality, traits such as your astuteness, curiosity, educational preferences, empathy, extrovertedness and introvertedness, resiliency, stubbornness, timeliness, your thinking style, etc. It also relates to your physical makeup and DNA.

Your blood type, eye color, hair color, height, etc.

Extrinsic characteristics are more so products of nature and nurture such as the way you dress, wear your hair, and accessorize yourself. They are reflective of your social skills and speaking style, your interest in things such as athletics, business, design, and music. It goes hand-and-hand with factors like your personal beliefs and moral code.

2. **Faith:** Whether you believe in God, gods, the universe, the Law of Attraction, no formal deity, are agnostic, or find yourself in another school of thought, your faith is an important aspect of your personal brand. For this context, I am not referring to a person's faith in themselves or another person, instead the faith that determines and influences their belief system and their outlook on life.

Without a sense of purpose, nihilism and internal chaos can manifest. Philosophers throughout the years such as Nietzsche have questioned faith's role in our civilization, some arguing that it was only necessary to establish civilization and dictate what are now commonly accepted laws such as *"Thou shall not murder,"* and *"Thou shall not steal."* As much as I love theology when this discussion arises, I would like to stay focused on the importance of faith in terms of your personal brand. As I mentioned at the beginning of this Manifesto, personal branding is what established some of the most widely practiced religions from Christianity to Islam, and Buddhism to Sikhism. Faith, or the lack thereof, remains a pillar of your personal brand. Faith allows you to connect to others at the deepest levels of humanity.

Earlier in my career, I made the argument that when it comes to your personal brand, you do not need to make it known where your faith stands. I bunched it up into the same category as politics and viewed it as wise to avoid doing things that can divide your audience or make people feel excluded. When it comes to faith today and through my observations, it is more important than ever to not make exclamations of faith in a way to disregard or categorize people, but rather as a firm statement of your own personal standing. If people can be aware of your background and what has influenced you into becoming the person you are, they are more likely to trust and understand you. In becoming a person of public relevance, do not do things that would disparage your faith or make you look hypocritical. For example, if you find and label yourself as a conservative Christian, it might not be wise to go out to bars and drink on a weekly basis. It is much better to be a good practitioner of your faith and simply show it in a way that does not tout ego.

3. **Personal Beliefs:** Depending on your faith journey, your personal beliefs have probably been widely influenced by your religious standing. Your personal beliefs are also nurtured into you by your parents. If you grew up in a household that was generally Republican, in relation to the United States of America, you either share many of those same tenants today or have cast them aside entirely. Your work ethic was instilled by your environment. Even your timeliness may

depend on if your parents were always late as an adult or always arrived early.

Your beliefs on how you should act and how society should function as a whole is a byproduct of the circumstances from your childhood alongside who you've been involved with as an adult and the influence they have had on you. What are your personal beliefs in terms of politics? What are your stances on openly discussed issues? Do you believe in capitalism or socialism? Do you believe in the right to choose? Do you feel that business people who make billions of dollars are horrible human beings or that they contribute to society? What is your stance on taxes? Should they be increased or lowered? This list could extend for pages because that is the kind of being humans are. Our complexity has layers of beliefs and within those beliefs, they have been dictated and influenced by a wide range of experiences and triggers.

I do not expect you to list out every single belief that you have, but having a generalized idea of what you stand for and what you don't, helps you determine how you would like to be perceived by the broader public and manage associations. Our faith allows us to come across with more nuance and vigor. I would suggest that you find opportunities to get into the public eye that allows you to show that deeper side of yourself and communicate more than one-sided perspectives. Showcasing your complexity gives people layers to dive into and makes you appear much more interesting; this is the art of storytelling.

4. **Profession:** The most self-explanatory of these five factors, your profession is what people will come to you for in terms of a service that you can provide. It is also the combination of all of your previous work experience which has developed and made you the professional you are today.

   In *When You Lack Expertise or Skills [8.2]*, I talk about what to do when you don't yet have much experience, but remain set on becoming well-known and established in a particular field. You do not have to be the Number 1 leading expert to be positioned as a top expert or even remotely one of the best.

Your profession is the most tangible and straightforward aspect of your brand. It describes how you provide a solution to another's problem whether that be in the form of a product or service, and in exchange the other person is gratified and in many cases the world is better because of it.

You may be in the entertainment space and believe that you are not providing a solution, yet entertainment is just that. You are helping another person feel good through your acting, comedy, and content, etc;. Being a professional golfer is in terms of personal branding, equal to being a lawyer or a doctor. It doesn't matter what profession you find yourself in, it is all a part of who you are. If you are already retired, at one point you were a practicing professional and have years of industry experience to share. It is common for people to seek out those who have heightened experience in a specific area. If you're interested in marketing, you're going to search out marketers. If you'd like to get better at copywriting, you'll look for copywriters.

If you have yet to determine what career or profession you're pursuing, ask yourself: *"What do I want people to feel as they're following me?"* Is your future profession aimed towards entertainment or education? Is it B2B or B2C? In person or virtual? Without a profession, you rely heavily on your personality, but are limited in the reasons you are giving people to further back you.

5. **Hobbies:** The final factor relating to your personal brand are your hobbies. These are the activities that you particularly enjoy and have been engaging in for a period of time. Your business mentors are usually not so all-consumed that they don't have any hobbies. Maybe they enjoy going out to dinner on a Friday night, bicycling in nature, participating in triathlons, traveling the world, or going to plays. These extracurriculars make life more enjoyable to you. *Share them!*

T: List off all of the things that make you, YOU! Characteristics, Faith, Personal Beliefs, Profession and Hobbies. You will need to decide what you want to put on display in a later exercise.

4.3 | **Elevator Pitch**

Part of positioning your personal brand is in how you communicate it by voice. An *elevator pitch* is defined as how you would describe yourself to someone if you were only sharing a brief ride on an elevator. If you had less than a minute to get your point across what would you say?

To achieve long lasting relationships and create lasting impressions, you have to connect in more profound ways than just your profession. What are your signatures? Are you a coffee drinker? Are you somebody who drinks coffee black without sugar? You would be amazed at how many people will automatically like you that much more or question your liver health because you drink your coffee black. The simple fact that you, too, need your daily dose of caffeine as game fuel *(I do)*.

Your elevator pitch is not an opportunity for you to sell your products and services, rather it serves as an opportunity to sell yourself as someone to get to know or follow. By leaving a lasting impression of increase, the person on the receiving end will not easily forget about you. A lasting impression of increase is when the person you engage with leaves their interaction better or more knowledgeable than they were going into it. A feeling that they can believe, do, and think bigger. You do this by actively living the way I covered in the prior chapter on *Mindset [3]*.

From that moment of your introduction, find a way to stay in contact with them as there is no telling what mutually beneficial situations will arise from that random point of contact. More importantly, keep your elevator pitch concise and lead it into a conversation about the other person. I have provided an example of one of my elevator pitches I'd give in front of a group below:

Hey, it's great to connect with you! My name is Isaac Mashman and I almost always show up with a cup of coffee in hand, so I apologize in advance if I appear wired. I run a personal brand consulting firm, Mashman Consulting Group and specialize in helping emerging and established public figures optimize and scale their personal brands. I have also written several books on the subject, have my own podcast, and I travel and get paid to speak. I'd love to get to know you all on a more individual basis so feel free to spark a conversation after the meeting.

When we break down my pitch, you will see that it has a brief but humorous hook, a sentence to build rapport, a professional synopsis, and titles that immediately bolster my authority. At the end I put out a call to action to express my intent and simultaneously make everyone in the room more comfortable coming up to me.

It is an intentional value exchange.

T: Write your elevator pitch. It should have a personal hook and a professional punchline. Make it personable, but not salesy. After you are done, read it aloud several times. Polish as needed.

4.4 | **Rapport**

The five factors that make up your personal brand help you build rapport with others so that upon meeting somebody for the first time, they are on the path to move from being a stranger to an acquaintance, an acquaintance to a friend, and friend to a best friend. A step further and they might even go from being your best friend to what some would consider to be family. Rapport is defined as *a harmonious relationship*. Every fact about you can help you build rapport with another.

Rapport is built not just through the ways you are alike but also through time spent together, breaking bread together, introductions from other trusted sources, and from the media. All of the places where your story, words, and works are the subjects at hand. As your connections grow, look for shared interests while seeking ways in which you can provide value. Value does not always translate into a monetary transaction as you can be providing value in the form of *education*, *entertainment*, or by being *inspirational*.

Your personal brand should never solely rely on your professional traits. *Ensure your personality shows through.* Incorporate this into your *Elevator Pitch [4.3]* and your marketing as there is very little time to make a first impression and somebody mustn't get the wrong one. Building rapport is how you get someone to warm up to you and the degree of that you have with a person is expressed through the number of times they reach out to you to talk, ask you for advice, introduce you to their network, and promote your work. It is expressed in instinctive influence when favors are asked of them or during your launches.

Identical twins sharing the same DNA have entirely unique fingerprints. One twin may be interested in the arts and the other in sports. No one else has ever had our symbolic *"fingerprint"* on the world, or the blend of our past experiences, thoughts, and influences that make up our identity. Pinpointing your unmistakable character traits and interests is a way to subsidize on your *uniqueness*. Capitalizing on your individuality is a great way of establishing rapport with people who share similar interests and strengthens your relationships with people who are genuinely interested in learning more about you.

Take a couple of minutes and list out things such as your hobbies, your interests, and your quirks, regardless of how small or large they might be and hold on to that list. There will come a point where you are able to tell a story from experience, talk about what occupies your time outside of your profession, and really showcase the person behind the public persona. Reality TV stars have full-blown shows with budgets of millions of dollars built around extended looks into that person's life from their skincare & makeup routine, to their wardrobes, to how they interact with their family members. Occasionally letting others have a look into your lifestyle will pique the interest of the public.

Remember that although we live in a transactional society, not all transactions have a face value.

Q: How have you built rapport with your friends in the past? What about your friendships make them work, in comparison to the colleague or family member you find yourself at odds with?

4.5 | **Avoiding Clichés**

It is known by now that I am addicted to coffee. I probably drink a little too much and drink it too late into the night contrary to what health experts recommend. When I sit down for a podcast interview or go to speak on stage I'll often have a cup of coffee in hand or close by. I use it as a way to break the ice, as discussed in the subchapter *Elevator Pitch [4.3]*, as a way to build rapport. I've aligned myself in such a way that if somebody wanted to give me a gift to catch my attention all they would need to do would be bring me coffee or a nice bag of roasted coffee beans.

This is something that is not wholly unique to me as millions of people around the world also share my addiction, yet, holds enough novelty that I have attached myself to it without making it my professional brand as a coffee bean salesman. It is an authentic part of my life but does not come across as cliché.

Read the following sentences: *"The secret to success is consistency! All you need to do is hustle! Motivation is essential!"* Word vomit we have all heard before.

People rely on clichés when they have nothing better to say or cannot find the ingenuity within their spirit to come up with something original. What do those phrases teach you? Absolutely nothing and as discussed in the next section, the reasons why content is consumed are: *education, entertainment, motivation,* and *connection.* A cliché does little for someone aside from making you come across as desperate.

It doesn't matter how much truth is found in a specific cliché, like that found in *"Consistency is important and you cannot achieve success without being motivated or disciplined."* It ultimately lacks any degree of depth. It isn't teaching something new or gets them to take action.

There is a massive difference between providing value and providing what I refer to as *strategic value.* The motivational speaker who wants to get on stage and grow their career as the person who is the motivator has to operate with nuance. Maybe they take some of their past trauma and are using it to propel them. Their biggest disadvantage is now their advantage. If they're going up on stage and talking about staying motivated despite hardships, are they repeating the same pieces of information or are they sharing specific examples about a circumstance in their life and what they were able to learn from it?

Jim Davidson was on Mount Everest during one of the most dangerous days in its history. Nineteen people died, and dozens of people were injured. I remember his speech on resiliency at the Atlantic-Oase Professional Conference more than I ever anticipated I would.

He didn't start his speech by saying *"Be resilient"* and left it at that. Sure, it may have led to a temporary moment of motivation in the hearts of the people in attendance, but that would have been it. Be resilient! Awesome—how memorable. Instead, he spent the entirety of his speech, telling the exact story and what was going on, not only in his mind, but also in the minds of others at Base Camp. He gave the exact steps they took as they traversed across ravines and thousand foot drops. He shared the raw video footage of when he was in his tent, questioning and wondering if he would end up dying. His speech, for being such a cliché topic as resiliency, deeply resonated with the audience because of how touching and personable he made it. *The context mattered.*

As you're building your personal brand and experiencing dull moments, you may not feel inspired to create anything at all or share your daily life. Resorting to clichés may seem like a good idea under these situations, but let me ask you, is that cliché going to do anything positive for your personal brand? This is one of those instances where I would say that relying on your *factory settings* of using something that you've heard a million times could harm your personal brand as it shows that you do not have what it takes to think for yourself.

The phrase, *"Your personal brand is the most important thing you can build"* will become a cliché. We already see it starting with the rise of uncertified and unmerited personal brand coaches, agencies, and consultants. It is my hope that through this Manifesto and my continued work, I introduce complexity to the subject and demonstrate why it's important in detailed mannerisms.

The personal branding space is becoming increasingly competitive and these repetitive phrases can only be used by so many people, so many times. Everyone will know that if they want to make more money, they need to grow their personal brand. If they want more influence, they need to grow their personal brand. Understanding that the market is set up for saturation, do you think that clichés will be the thing that helps me cut through the noise? *Originality and cleverness is and will be.*

If you do choose to come across as cliché on occasion or use one in your materials, expand on it. Talk about why it is relevant and approach it with complexity. Break it down so it can be understood by bringing up information that pertains to deepening your point. *A position of authority versus a jester set up for mockery.*

Q: What is something unique to you that others may find interesting or quirky? What fun facts about you potentially make you stand apart?

4.6 | **Leaning Into Your Name**

You might find it surprising to know that I hated my last name for the longest time. Being raised by a single mom and my grandparents I didn't have any contact with my biological father until I was already an adult. I'm grateful that today I have a wonderful relationship with him but as a child anything that was associated with my father, I perceived negatively.

There were moments when I considered taking the last name of my maternal grandfather or changing it to something different altogether. To make matters worse, the name *Mashman* has a semblance to mashed potatoes and all other mash-related labels. It was the subject of bullying in my early years as students can be cruel. In retrospect, the bullying was never awful as far as bullying is concerned, but it deepened my hatred towards the name. In my senior year of high school, I began to realize that in having such an unusual name, it could be used to my benefit. I wasn't having to fight with other people to secure my social media handles or purchase my domain. If you ran a search at the time, nothing popped up outside of DNA and genealogy websites.

The thing that I hated turned out to be one of my biggest gifts. In my work with clients, regardless of the industry, I find that many people are not blessed with such a gift. Their first name might be more common such as John or Sarah, therefore presenting an uphill battle for visibility and against others who share similar spellings. If you are one of the people who were given an uncommon name at birth you should certainly lean into it, however, if you're one of the many people who weren't, I would recommend potentially incorporating your middle name.

Several years ago an audio engineer and friend of mine approached me for help. After running several searches I very quickly found out that the name Tristan Roberts was shared by professional skiers and even politicians. I told him in a brutally honest way, that he would not be able to compete with public figures such as this for visibility. I asked him, *"Tristan, what is your middle name?"* After queuing more searches, I consulted him that he should incorporate his middle name into all of his branding and marketing. He is no longer known as Tristan Roberts but as Tristan T. Roberts. I always provide this example with my clients as today he dominates the search and is building a memorable personal brand. Tristan has gone on to earn multiple Golden and Platinum plaques for his audio engineering work.

Whether you decide to use the initial of your middle name or the middle name in its entirety is up to you. Do some research on what shows up for both of the searches and repeat your name aloud to see if it rolls off of the tongue. Come to a decision that you think will be the most beneficial for you in your future successes. Also ensure that you would be able secure the social media handles and purchase your URL domain *(www.)* for a future website. You ideally want to see very little, if any search results for your name.

If you are somebody like me who has never cared for your name, this is your indicator that you should accept it for what it is and then run with it. Don't worry about people being able to pronounce it or if they'll love it. *You are the person who gives it relevance and power.*

T: Take the time to research your name. If you are competing with others, redirect your searches to include your middle name. Decide today whom YOU want to be known as.

4.7 | **Perception and Mystery**

Now that you have listed out and identified varying aspects of your being, how much do you make public and how much do you hide? How do you strike a healthy balance—*Is there a balance?* After the chapter on *Personal Skills [7]*, you'll be able to read the academic paper I published, *Identity Positioning: A Macroscopic View on Personal Branding [i]*. In it, I introduced a proprietary strategy called the Skyline Strategy, and although it is targeted specifically towards social media content, it establishes a healthy boundary for how you can maintain a good professional image while also showcasing some of those more personal and intimate aspects. For every two pieces of business content produced, i.e, what helps progress your business or profession, you publish one personal piece of content for a **2:1** ratio.

I'd extend this strategy to apply to topic ideas and actions in general. For every two actions you take that will help your business or career, take one action for yourself and personal interests. Artists will go years without publishing a new work, and musicians can go as long as decades before their next album comes out. Many of these people have established success already, but there is a shroud of mystery that covers what they are doing. By leaning into this mystery, you are building hype for a major release or upcoming projects and are essentially employing mystery as a marketing tool. If you were writing a book, you shouldn't tell every single person you meet the name of every single chapter. You have to leave room for discovery. As I hike in the woods, I prefer to explore the surrounding area myself. I don't need to see photographs of every trail or every tree, as *I want to experience it.*

Mystery is what makes it interesting. If everyone already knew the answer, why would they ever hire you as a professional? They wouldn't! Mystery and the invocation of curiosity are what lead to action and you need to develop your personal brand in such a way that gets people to come back for more because they're intrigued.

Think about how we perceive ultra-successful billionaires. We have witnessed Amazon's Jeff Bezos get into better shape and start living a billionaire lifestyle just as we have seen Mark Zuckerberg of Meta and Facebook train jiu-jitsu. We may not know everything, but we know just enough to stay interested. As you lead up to the launch of a new business, a significant investment, or something noteworthy, begin hinting at it, but don't share all of the details. You could submit a press release and promote it, make a post, send an email, or do some other gimmick but make it appealing. Your personal brand is yours and the degree of privacy that you are willing to sacrifice should be done meticulously and methodically.

Don't share something without an intention behind it. If you're going out to dinner and want to make a post of your meal, ask yourself *why*. Does it show your affluence? Your palette? Is it your first post back after a hiatus that serves as a check-in? There must be a reason. As your fame and influence grow, it's a good practice to make it a habit of posting the places you've been after you've already left as a safety precaution.

Perception and mystery also produces speculation. The larger your personal brand becomes, so does your perceived value. In the markets, money is made off of speculation. Is the market going up or is the market going down? We are always speculating about something and this can be seen in the entertainment industry with actors. Actors can demand more based on their previous works. Has an actor been part of a blockbuster movie before this one? If they have, we assume that this movie will automatically perform better than that of a C-list figure. An artist who's charted before is likely to chart again. These two examples share something in common, too. They aren't sharing all of their secrets.

A personal brand built around capability and reliability suggests that prior results are bound to happen again.

A: Before you make an announcement, begin to hint at it during media appearances, in your content, and in messaging. Build up some suspense leading to the launch.

4.8 | **Inspiration vs. Copying**

They say that imitation is the highest form of flattery. There have been multiple instances of people taking how I phrase a certain call to action (CTA) and applying it to their material. I'm never offended by this, but I would prefer they work with me as a client than just take what I do. I have no issue with somebody being inspired by my actions and putting their spin on it, but when it is verbatim, *the exact copy,* it rubs me the wrong way. As you are reverse engineering your mentors or someone whose strategy you want to apply, it shouldn't look like you did so. If you copy someone too aggressively and who is widely known, and it appears as such, people will doubt you for your originality, and it can actually affect your reputation in a negative way.

Your personal brand is about you, and I would put forth the challenge to take the extra time to make it seem and sound like such. Your personal brand is personal! It's almost like when a well-known fast food chain creates an advertisement and then a mom-and-pop shop uses the same color scheme and font to construct their own. It loses that familial feeling that keeps people coming back to the restaurant. Imagine if that mom-and-pop restaurant took its marketing strategy and where they posted that advertisement and instead crafted a personalized ad that spoke to the history and story of the establishment. It would be so much more effective.

Take inspiration from the strategy and use the very best from it, but do not copy its aspects that are easy to change. Those of you who are just starting out are especially susceptible because you feel like you have to copy somebody else to get a leg up. This is not the case. Don't come across as a try-hard, but as somebody who is crafty, cool, calm, and collected. I believe that you can do so much more for your personal brand by reverse engineering what works and putting your personal electric flare to it.

A: Mimic a successful campaign or strategy of another public figure, either in business, social media, or otherwise. Put your unique spin on it and evaluate the response. For example, take a piece of viral content and rephrase it to apply to your personal brand.

4.9 | **Gimmicks and Creativity**

Too much flare can be a bad thing. When I mention gimmicks, I am not referring to creative marketing crutches like loyalty programs, calling out competitors, or guerrilla marketing tactics. In terms of your personal brand when I say *gimmick*, I am referring to being the person who dresses up as Willy Wonka and performs magic tricks. Goofy analogy, but a real one. I remember several years ago when I was flown out to Washington DC for Facebook's Meta-Boost Gather event, one of the small business owners came dressed in a full-blown Willy Wonka costume. I am by no means trying to disrespect what he does for a profession as he is genuinely a good guy, but to me, and to this day, he comes across as a gimmick.

In lieu of creating his own identity as a magician and being taken seriously, he relies on being Willy Wonka. He has the top hat, a cane like Gene Wilder, a bright purple blazer, and carries around a golden chocolate bar in his pocket. That is what I mean by gimmick.

As you're building out your personal brand, being creative and attaching certain things to your public persona, such as a certain kind of attire, a way of speech, an opening message for your videos, or a closing statement are all ways that contribute to your public identity. Whether you decide to always start a video with a cup of coffee in hand like I usually do, composing a recognizable marketing *"scheme"* for your personal brand like a game show-themed podcast, or taking photos with every new person you meet, creativity makes it so people come back time and time again, and more importantly, they stay.

Q: Can you think of someone who came across as a gimmick? Did it make you feel more or less confident in their abilities?

4.10 | **Shaping Your Image**

As extensive the chapter *Mindset [3]* was, all of the information I referenced is quintessential to developing the tools needed to shape your personal brand's image. From *Becoming the 1% [3.1]*, to understanding *Burnout [3.6]*, and Analysis Paralysis, my hope is that in time you are able to properly chisel away at your personal brand and consequently yourself as the individual so you can better optimize your reputation, how you're viewed, and your performance.

Shaping Your Image is as much about developing who you are as a human being as it is expressing who you are to those looking in on you. Mediocrity is not respected, but excellence is. You'll occasionally notice that your personal brand is leaning in one direction, such as one of the titles that you gave yourself, when you actually want to be known for something else. When this happens, you'll need to stop promoting one subject and introduce another. If you have been rigorously promoting your book for the last 12 months, and now want to bring more attention to your business, you'll take a step back from marketing yourself as an author and start talking about your expertise and offers. Use your book as a way to establish credibility for your service or product, but make it commonly accepted that you are a business owner, first and foremost. You will likely have multiple things that you are working on, but won't want to be known for all of them.

As you're developing your personal branding strategy, understand that every action you are taking is contributing to your personal brand and that the smallest of efforts are shaping your image. Look for flaws or cracks in your foundation that you could spend time improving and tweaking. During my consultations with clients, I often come across as tedious or obsessive when I point out a space or comma where there shouldn't be. A period next to *Mr.* appears better than *"Mr"* — *Appearance influences judgement.*

At least once a month audit your personal brand and look for the following metrics:

1. **Seamless Branding:** I.e, the same marketing message and appearance across all platforms or vehicles; ensure you have remained consistent.

2. **Omnipresence:** The establishment of a personal brand that is visible everywhere, all the time and attracts opportunities. This can

be measured based on how many places and platforms your name is showing up. Articles, blogs, directories, mentions, podcasts, so on.

3. ***Momentum Report:*** A measurement of your community engagement, how many people are contacting you, quantity of attracted opportunities, etc:. You should also be checking for negative comments or stories to help gauge and determine what you need to change or look out for moving forward.

Be proactive in your evolution. If the biography that you wrote several months ago no longer reflects what you are doing today, update it! If you've gotten more photos taken from the last time you changed your media kit, include those new photos! Reverse engineer what has worked for other people in the past. This calls for working backward from a point of success. How did they get their start? What worked and what didn't? Make it your aim to understand what they did that yielded outcomes both positive and negative, and if they are alive take heed to their present branding and marketing. Don't become them, but take the best aspects of their strategy, put your own touches to it, and execute on this newly found plan. *What early opportunities did they pursue?*

In your process, say yes to a lot of things until it becomes more beneficial to say no and be aware of where you are spending your time. Reverse engineering is not about stealing anything, it's about observing and applying the very best. *You're not copying them in so much as you're learning from them.*

My earliest days of building my personal brand were spent researching my mentors. I looked for things such as: what social media platforms they were active on, what channels they distributed their materials, the places they were interviewed, the kind of profile pictures they used, the custom email addresses they chose for themselves and their teams, and even how they incorporated their homes into their materials. I eventually saw trends develop and adopted my findings to my own personal brand.

T: Take this time to examine your personal brand as it is today. Is your material up to date? What from your past messaging no longer applies? Make changes where needed.

4.11 | **Deliverables**

Your personal brand is comparable to a business that has deliverable products and services. If you think about the kind of content that people are consuming, there are four overarching *benefits* or *reasons* that they are consciously or more commonly, subconsciously looking for. They can be *Entertained, Educated, Motivated/Inspired,* and *Connected* to the creator. These effectively act as your deliverables to the person on the consuming end.

As rapport develops over time, a degree of brand loyalty and the expectation that comes along with your name will eventually develop as well. If you have been on the creating end for an extended period, have various professional accolades, and a certain number next to your follower count, then your reputation has already been built and what is expected of you is increased in parallel. The quality of which you produced several years ago is not the quality you're expected to be producing today.

The comedian should always be working to come up with new material as jokes can only be told so many times before they get overplayed. Educators need to continuously expand their own knowledge so they can share more relevant information or revise their facts. The person who is living a lifestyle or serving as the motivator must remain motivated themselves or talk about the times that they are not and what they have experienced.

Content generates rapport and instills the following in the minds of those who know you: *confidence in your abilities, confidence in referring you to their own network,* and *confidence in offering endorsements* or *desiring to collaborate with you.* You want to be the person that others want to collaborate with because they know and have an expectation in their mind of potential outcomes. It is the mental association people have with larger than life figures that gives them the runway to charge hundreds of thousands of dollars, whereas the person who is starting out might only be able to charge a couple of hundred. Deliverables are seen in different ways and when you understand the complexity of this, you'll also come to appreciate every small accomplishment and its role relative to your progress.

Q: What are you delivering through your personal brand? For example, if you're educating others, what are some of the exact takeaways through your materials?

4.12 | **Colors and Personal Branding**

Like Mcdonald's is red and yellow, or Ford Motors is blue, you have to develop a seamless brand with a consistent color scheme. For my own personal brand, I strategically chose to use white and black to portray that corporate executive, but clean and contemporary feel when somebody visits my page and related works; the cover of this book is black and white, consistent with my branding. This reflects in the colors of clothing I wear, the photos I take, and the marketing materials and graphics I have for my podcast. *It was all intentional.*

Depending on the color, there are different emotions that will be communicated and reflected. Red is traditionally used for sales and calls to action, green gives you a sense of growth and money, whereas blue is passive and peaceful. *What do you want your personal brand to appear as?* These are things that you need to be considering if you want to scale your personal brand and foster a professional image. If you are always wearing pastels and neutral colors, but your marketing materials are bright red, is that a proper representation of your personal brand? There must be strategic planning on your part from the color of the shirt you wear in the morning, to the email you designed and sent.

Celebrities pay thousands of dollars for stylists that help them choose their outfits. They wear select brands which align with the image they want to maintain and reflect their collaborations and given endorsements. You do not have to go out and hire a stylist of your own, but next time you go shopping make conscious buying decisions and choose clothing that suits your personal brand. At the minimum, apply this subchapter for the benefits it will have on your mindset. Your competitors aren't thinking about matching their outfits to their posts or website. *Details matter!*

T: Research the associations and meaning behind your favorite colors. Pick two colors to begin using for your personal brand. If they are too contrasting and don't work well together, choose another.

4.13 | **Audio Branding**

A less commonly known form of branding is that of *Audio Branding*. This is where a jingle, song, or voice is associated with a brand. Think about some of the most common commercials that you've seen on television or heard on the radio. They're catchy, promotional materials that get stuck in your head. I'm not suggesting that you have to have your own custom-made song to be associated with your personal brand, but if you choose to host your own podcast, or record videos that have an introduction, think about how you are sounding. Come up with something that *forces your image to stand out*.

If you are filming vlogs around your life, having the same tune for the first minute or using it throughout, will get people accustomed to your style of content. Professionally managed podcasts have *"intros"* and *"outros"* where either the host or another person is talking and over time the listeners can expect to hear that every time they tune in. Do you want your personal brand to sound dark and melancholy, cheerful and hopeful, reflect a certain genre such as hip hop or country?

This form of branding is especially significant for public speakers as their voice is their power. When was the last time you heard yourself? Take 5 minutes to record a voice memo where you're talking to an imaginary group about something you love. Listen back to the audio and pay special attention to how you sound. Is the memo full of filler words such as *"uh," "like,"* and *"but?"* Do you sound confident and are you changing the intonations of your voice to express emotion? Not only is this a good exercise to gauge how well you are speaking, it also gives you a chance to hear what others do and step into their shoes.

A: Get comfortable with your voice. Experiment with it and take ownership of how you sound. Understand your tonalities, how you can inflect emotions, command attention, etc. Recording yourself speaking or listening to past media is encouraged. Eliminate filler words and points of contest when you can.

4.14 | **The Art of Storytelling**

What is a story that you often find yourself repeating? The kind of story that you tell your friends or family, like a funny mistake, something significant from your childhood or other odds and ends. Have you ever *(obviously depending on the context)* considered telling that story to your audience? One of the absolute best ways of building rapport using your personal brand is through sharing stories from your own life. Once you've been interviewed a couple dozen times, you will get into the flow of being able to answer the question *"Who are you?"*

You will understand pivotal points based on the interviewer's response, the shock factor, and using introspection. When I first started in the Network Marketing industry, mind you I am no longer involved and haven't been for years, one of the biggest parts of selling was sharing stories from my upbringing. The fact that I was raised in a single parent home, saw my mom working low-paying jobs, didn't have money for all of the niceties and things in life that we would've preferred, etc. I used my story as a way to set the vision for what I was chasing in that business opportunity and to build rapport.

After I left the industry, I took my experience in sales and applied it towards my interviews. I narrowed in on what I wanted to mention based on the purpose it was serving. Talking about my grandparents and the roof caving in and black mold in the bedroom connected emotionally and sharing how I was a straight-A student who decided not to pursue college portrayed the magnitude of the risk I took by pursuing a career in business.

It is through storytelling that people continued to support me despite my fickleness as I went from business to business until I eventually wound up in the personal branding space. That often surprised me as I would go six months in one industry, just to jump to another, yet people would not unfollow me because they were there for me—*for Isaac Mashman*. If you only talk about your profession, you lack that personal hook and therefore that relationship is going to be one-sided. *People will only stick around to see what they can get from you.*

Storytelling does not have to be from your past. As you're living life, traveling, and doing great things as I know you will, let people in on what you have going on. Talk about your most recent trip; was it for business or was it for family? If you're going on a run, consider taking a photo of the scenery or recording an impromptu video. There is no need to share your bathroom routine and display it for the world to see, but cut through some of that mysterious cloud surrounding your personal brand and let people know who *you* are. In doing so, you can interact with your audience and ask them questions in a free flowing manner like: *"Have you ever experienced XYZ? Let me tell you about a story from my life..."* Even if you're not asking the question using a medium that allows them to share their responses, it engages the person on the other end and in many cases, bolsters their enthusiasm.

Q: What is YOUR story? If you were put on the spot right now, where would you start? What aspects are important and worth mentioning?

4.15 | **1st, 2nd, and 3rd Person**

I'm not expecting to replace your English teacher, or give you some boring lesson, but based on who you are talking to, you should use the proper point of view. Businesses will use a mix of third and second person POVs for their corporate websites, descriptions, and marketing. They say *"we"* and *"our."* We don't see the top companies saying *"I want."*

Using the first person point of view such as *"I am"* infers that you are sharing a story or communicating how you feel. Whenever you're making a call to action, by combining a first person POV with second person, you can come up with effective pitches such as: *"I would love for you to follow me on xyz platform."* This makes it appear as a personal favor and speaks directly to them. Rotating perspectives induces the communal feeling that the subject at hand is larger than you.

Remember the analogy to fire? The people are your oxygen that breathes life into your personal brand. You don't want to talk about yourself all the time, instead include others in your endeavors and mission. When you end your professional punchline don't redundantly say *"I help people,"* consider saying *"I help you!"* notice how the dynamic shifts?

You're approaching it out of service rather than ego. When referring to your business, say *"We."* Your business is a separate entity that exists on its own. For example:

Through Mashman Consulting Group, we help emerging and established public figures optimize and scale their personal brands.

The alternative would be in first person:

I help emerging and established public figures optimize and scale their personal brands.

The first phrase is communal, showing that the business consists of more than one person and would be used for material exclusive to MCG, whereas the second phrase is singular and would be used for my personal brand. *For the business owners who are reading this, whatever you do,* **please do not use your business pages and platforms for personal purposes!**

Q: What situations would you use 1st, 2nd, and 3rd person points of view for your personal brand?

4.16 | **Seamless Branding**

Seamless Branding is achieved through the consistent and maintained portrayal of yourself. There should be no doubt who you are when someone is introducing you, both on and offline, and likewise, there should be no question you are the right person to subscribe to. It starts by defining *what you want to be known for* and figuring out *who you are*. The subsequent steps are relatively straightforward:

1. **Run a Search on Your Name:** Google is the current search engine of significance and will likely remain so for years to come. Do you show up or are you on the 10th page? If you're fighting other people who share your name apply the principles discussed under the subchapter *Leaning Into Your Name [4.6]. You can* incorporate your middle name either by initial or in its entirety and you will want to purchase your domain URL, secure the same social media handles across every relevant platform, and begin being introduced and introducing yourself as such. You're not John Doe, you're *John* <u>*Zechariah*</u> *Doe* or *John* <u>*Z.*</u> *Doe.*

If you look at my own personal brand you will see I own *Isaacmashman.com* and can be found everywhere *@isaacmashman*. I did this early on as I wanted to ensure I was discoverable. I do not personally use my middle names as I'm not competing with other Isaacs, but if you do not have that blessing, I'd advise you to incorporate your own.

2. **Use the Same Pictures:** This is referring to profile pictures, headshots, and header images. You want others to become familiar with how you look and have no question about the identity of who they're following. I'd encourage you to have a collection of photos for various use cases and as a general rule, try your best to not use the same photo twice. Sure, it requires more work, but it creates a compilation of media that can be used for interviews, promotional materials, your website, and more.

3. **Use the Same Marketing Message:** As it stands today my marketing message is *"Addicted to coffee and standards. I help*

emerging and established public figures optimize and scale their personal brands." Based on the space available for headlines I may add in titles like *Author, Business Owner, Investor, Podcast host* while if there is less space, I'll shorten it to say: *"Addicted to coffee. I help public figures optimize and scale their personal brands."* Notice the personal hook and professional punchline.

Based on the platform's primary demographic I may edit my biography to be more formal or personalized but what I am communicating stays the same—long-form biographies included.

4. **A Consistent Tone:** Don't change the way you speak from platform-to-platform. Who you are is what people will know you for. It may not be wise to post a raw video of you cursing on a professional networking site, but you could always post the censored, edited version. I'll delve into what you should and should not share in the following chapter *Reputation Management [5].*

Crafting a seamless personal brand makes it easy to find, understand, and support you. Confusing your audience is the last thing you want and having mismatched messaging does just that.

Having a seamless brand contributes to your personal brand becoming *omnipresent*. Omnipresence is typically used when referring to God, as God is everywhere all the time. In the least sacrilegious way possible, I am here to tell you to aim to do the same with your personal brand. You should be visible and discoverable, whenever and wherever possible. You want to be able to tell someone *"Look me up if you want to learn more!"* Imagine the authority that is conveyed by dominating the search engines. *Instant credibility.*

T: Perform another audit of your personal brand. At first glance, does it appear seamless? Try your best to be impartial and put yourself in the shoes of a complete stranger. What do you see that is working and what could be better?

| 5 |

Reputation Management

It is as much about keeping and maintaining your reputation, as it is building it

Your reputation is an aspect of your personal brand but *it is not your personal brand*. Reputation is the general consensus surrounding a subject.

Is that consensus positive or negative?

Is there trust or concern?

Authority or mediocrity?

As we previously discussed, your personal brand consists of your characteristics and personality, your ability to deliver results and add to the lives of others, your skills and profession, your accomplishments and failures, and so on. It all contributes to the composition of your reputation.

Reputation is also relative to your surroundings. How your friends and family perceive you will vastly differ from that of your fellow professionals. A doctor may have a pristine reputation as a surgeon and be granted assumed authority, but alone their reputation doesn't necessarily translate to massive exposure. If that doctor were to take their knowledge and skills and proceed to connect with a wider group through methods such as: *contributing to highly regarded medical journals, co-authoring studies* and *papers, making morning television appearances,* or *writing a book,* they could easily broaden their reputation's reach. In doing so, they may go from *"anybody's doctor,"* to the sought after surgeon that the most affluent want for their procedures or the researcher who donors appear to throw money at.

5.1 | Leaning Tower

In the story of David and Goliath *(1 Samuel Ch. 17),* Goliath's demise was caused by the conceited belief he was too big to fall. How could a shepherd armed with just a sling, possibly kill a Philistine warrior, let alone a warrior who was also a giant? There are many lessons on personal branding and reputation management we can take from this Biblical account. It all started before the fateful day David visited the creek bed to pick his stones and walked into the enemy camp. Goliath had established a reputation as a fierce soldier, his stature and size of which surely invoked fear and made for better wartime storytelling. He became egotistical in every definition of the word and went as far as mocking the Israelites and God. As his leaders warred against King Saul, he issued a one-on-one challenge against anyone so bold. David, feeling an obligation to defend his God, put an end to the Philistine's blasphemy and with the whip of his arm and the force of the sling, the giant fell. It is said that the army was so discouraged by the event, they fled.

Goliath's reputation was tarnished.
David's had just begun.

I share this story to serve as a warning. No matter how big you become or how far your personal brand's fame and influence reaches, you are always a single misstep away from it all crashing down.

It takes a single person who had a negative experience with you, personally or professionally, to start rumors and bring others in on your private matters. A single employee who begins talking negatively about their employer, plants seeds of doubt in their fellow workers' mind that eventually destroy the organization's culture and outward brand from within. In any case, addressing the issues as swiftly and intelligently as possible is a large part of damage control. If your foundation is not strong, your personal brand and everything you have worked hard for will *fall like a house of cards*.

Which is more dangerous, one cancer cell, or the accumulation of millions that form the tumor? All cancer starts with one mutation and if certain interactions go unchecked and false or negative rumors spread, they can be cancerous for your personal brand. Here are four of the ways you can respond:

1. **The Path of Accountability:** You recognize your mistakes and work to come to a resolution. By taking accountability you're able to prevent the cancer from spreading, but also admit to wrongdoing. Some will gain respect for you while others, no matter what you say or do, will forever have a negative perspective.

2. **Denial:** This occurs when you deny any and all allegations. If you deny an allegation and play the hardball route just to be proven wrong, it can result in more damage when compared to taking *The Path of Accountability*.

3. **Resolution Without Resolve:** When you take accountability, but the other party is too stubborn, hurt, or *"far gone"* to work with you. If you attempt to make things right, you're at least able to demonstrate to the public that you're working to fix what happened to the best of your abilities.

4. **Complete Ignorance:** You neither confirm nor deny any rumor and act as if you don't know a thing about it. This option may communicate that you are above small issues, or simply think you're better. It temporarily limits the rumor's exposure as you're not directly telling more people about it.

Each of these options have their pros and cons that should be factored before making any decision but remember that it was David's single act of faith that hit Goliath squarely between the eyes.

Q: If presented with a controversy, what path do you think you'd be the most prone to choose? Why?

5.2 | **Who Has Leverage Over You?**

This thinking is not meant to come across as Machiavellian or manipulative, but as proactive. One wrong move can uproot your entire life and ruin your reputation and potential opportunities with it. From the person who is recorded acting a fool while drunk, to the executive that sends crude photos to the wrong person. It is the celebrity that acts up in public and punches the phone out of a paparazzi's hand or the politician that makes a scene by getting belligerent on a plane. To be a public figure requires the understanding that you are being watched and that your actions are going to be scrutinized.

As your efforts begin to pay off, your downfall will come at a higher cost. Those with malicious intent will begin to view you and your success as a way for them to figuratively *"get a leg up."* This is where blackmail enters the equation as now you are somebody worth blackmailing, defined as *using an item or words with ill-intent to receive something in return.*

I would not recommend writing the following exercise out, and if you do make sure to shred the paper, but think about the different people throughout your life who might have leverage over you. Would these people ever use it against you?

We would hope not, but humans are fickle and circumstances can prove quite influential to upholding a person's moral compass.

Influence is a burden that forces and requires an individual to behave differently. To act with righteousness and keep the right company. If you portray yourself as a *"big shot"* business person yet have massive debts, a creditor could unscrupulously disclose your debt, resulting in the general public viewing you as a fraud. Being in control of who has power over you is simply good business and in contrast, you may have some similar control over others. A business has leverage over their employees and if they wanted to, could fire anybody regardless of the cost to the person that they are firing.

Society is made up of different kinds of leverage. Stock traders use brokers to give them access to more funding and make it more lucrative for them in the short term, yet one bad trade that is placed with too much confidence can cause them to go bankrupt. Being cautious and conscious of leverage makes you a very effective *"trader"* of this currency known as influence.

In most cases, such as the ones that were mentioned at the beginning of the subchapter, it isn't worth bringing up a point of concern with somebody from your past, rather be aware of it in case it ever arises. There is a good chance that the person who recorded the drunk video of you might have forgotten it ever happened or stopped caring altogether.

The best way to avoid losing leverage is to be strict in your actions and not fall susceptible to temptations. As for creditors and debts, resolve them as quickly as possible so you can move forward with your personal brand free of additional stress being added to your already growing burden; being a public figure is enough work as it is.

A dissatisfied client has sway with your business' reputation. If they choose to make their dissatisfaction public, one negative review potentially turns prospective clients away from working with you. A client who had a positive experience, holds a similar but less *"gripping"* power as they are able to influence people *to work with you.* Reputation is about managing and expounding upon perceptions. In the case of the client who feels like they didn't get their money's worth or had a negative experience, confront it head on and offer to resolve it before they would ever get the chance to share their situation with the public.

For the author that produces a low-quality marketing book, your readers are going to express their opinions for other shoppers to read. Public speakers who do not deliver great speeches will find future engagements harder to land.

Thinking that you are too big to fail or fall is the exact thinking that leads to your detriment. I don't care if you have 5,000 positive reviews or endorsements from others that talk about how great you are and that you're an exceptional human being, treat every point of contest with the utmost importance.

Leverage is also found in the falsification of truth. The business guru who rents his Lamborghini and acts like a high-flyer treads a very fine line of what is honest and what is false. When they are discovered not to be as wealthy and financially sound as they first let on, their reputation and trust disappears. If government organizations find that they are misleading the people with whom they are selling, legal cases can be launched with precedent. Leverage in any form comes with a risk and it is simply better to be a good person, than to ever sacrifice your fortune, financially and otherwise, in foolish hopes of obtaining something you do not deserve.

Q: Who from your past has leverage over you? Are you prepared to deal with the fall out should it be levied against you?

5.3 | **It Can't Be Bought**

Thinking that you can buy your way into a positive reputation is a fool's way of thinking. Your reputation will only go so far if you choose the easy way out. Pay-to-win tactics are representative of the fact you are not good enough; otherwise, why would you have to convince others to pay attention using your dollars?

True authority figures are who they are and let their results speak for themselves. Never try to convince anybody that you are trustworthy or notable. I am proud to say that I have never paid out-of-pocket for any press feature. Why are you reading my book? Did I pay for you to read it? No. What led you to make this purchase? Was it my name? A relationship we previously had? Were there other positive reviews? Seeing the potential best seller tag or top new release in its category? An interest in the subject? A combination of all of the above? *My reputation is now working for me.*

Nothing I mentioned can be bought, and they're all factors that contribute to our decision making on a daily basis, personal branding wise as well as in general consumerism.

Don't let yourself be led on by those vanity metrics that would drive you to make a rash purchase that sacrifices your laurels in an attempt to boost or artificially bolster your credibility. I'd like to expand on the example I provided under the subchapter *The Dangers of Fame [3.7]* where I discussed being approached by the *"expert"* selling some sort of biz-op, bot-selling affiliate program. Bots are, in essence, fake accounts that do little more than contribute to your follower count; it's not like they provide genuine engagement or have networks of their own to share your content with. During our first call, he used the analogy of being at a bar and said something along the lines of, *"If you went up to a girl and had 2,000 followers or 100,000, which guy do you think she would go home with?"* — Not only was this example extremely disrespectful to women in that they would promiscuously sell their sexuality for clout, it also told me a lot about his own moral code...Or rather, the lack thereof. *He was selling fake vanity.*

It was a way for someone to feel better about themselves and in the process they are lying to the real people looking for genuine authority figures to interact with. Since then, the Federal Trade Commission (FTC), has begun cracking down on these unethical practices under the pretenses of false advertising. Unfortunately where there is opportunity, people with impatient ambition will also be found.

Another trope worthy of mentioning is the pay-to-win press opportunities. I will not mention any outlet by name as I don't want to get on their legal team's radar, however, in recent years there has been a surge in *"Press Professionals"* offering *"high-caliber"* articles and interviews in notable media publications. They claim to guarantee placement, given, it comes with a hefty price tag often in the thousands, or tens of thousands of U.S. dollars. Some who have bought from these gurus do not care as a boost to their credibility is a boost to their credibility, but some others did so with a sense of genuine optimism, not knowing it was wrong. As the adage goes, "*if it's too good to be true, it probably is.*" I myself have been able to land multiple quotes within a 12-month time frame by pitching legitimate journalists, to being invited on for radio interviews, and have been widely distributed in newspapers...**All without paying my way into any of them.**

Those pay-to-win press moguls have since been blacklisted from most of these publications and if they do it again and are caught, will have a likelihood of finding themselves in the FTC's cross hairs. These practices are a falsification of credentials, could be perceived as bribery, and is undisclosed advertising. I doubt the media outlets want this kind of scrutiny, besides, what kind of credible public figure needs to pay to be featured and what does it say about the outlet if those featured in it, paid?

So what is the solution? *Compounding.* In time and as your reputation spreads, a funny little thing known as compounding occurs and that's when the real fun begins.

Q: Have you ever followed someone and later realized they were engaged in dishonest or pay-to-win practices? How did that affect your perception of them and their credibility? How did you find out?

5.4 | **Building Credibility**

In many cases, credibility is automatically built as more people know about you but those numbers will only get you so far. Sure, you can have a couple thousand or a couple of million, but what's more important is how much those who follow you, *trust you*. Trust is the understanding that this person or entity has good intentions. That you can rely on the subject to follow through on their word and drive you to an intended end result; *the subject's claims are accurate*. There are many ways to build your credibility.

Like you have a reputation, so does every other person or brand you associate yourself with. Can there be exchanges in credibility through collaborations? Are you associating with the right people? Is it known that you are in exclusive social circles? Seeking out other top performers in your industry and being seen is a *public display of competence*. Aim for their platforms and think about ways you could do business together. A meaningful and equally simple public relations tactic to help you grow your credibility while also gaining wisdom.

Work to be in the 1% of your profession's leaders and never factor out testimonials and endorsements, both written and video, from people both large and small.

Spend some of your energy showcasing your personality in clever ways. Build your credibility by associating with entertainers or with those in contrasting fields; you would be amazed at what conversations arise from talking with someone of perceived *unlikeness*. Take the comedian that goes on a business podcast, or the business person that goes on stage with the comedian. Unusual collaborations do more than provide entertainment. They build rapport and give the otherwise uptight professional permission to lower their guard.

Become locally well known by shaking as many hands as possible and by getting people to organically talk about you. *Make your selfless intentions public.* The local real estate developer who adopts the platform of revitalizing impoverished areas, may find getting permits is not as challenging as they once thought as it aligns with their politicians agendas.

The more you are seen and open up about who you are and your story, the more rapport will be built. If you have done something newsworthy, let the media know about it. Get into articles, onto local stations, podcasts, and other forms of media that arise in the years to come.

Finding ways to build your credibility comes down to: **A) Visibility,** or how large of an opportunity it is, and **B) Edification,** the quality of endorsement you are receiving. Some outlets are superior to others but come with an increased challenge to being included. Top outlets may not allow the professional who is just starting out to contribute expert advice. For those who are widely regarded, these same outlets will break down doors to get them on as a contributor. Platforms hosted by vetted industry figureheads and that have monumental demographics won't just let anyone on.

If you are bold enough to approach your idols, do so as their equal as they will be much more receptive to hearing you out. *"Cassidy, I'm your biggest fan! Please let me interview you!"* vs. *"Cassidy, I loved what you did with X! I host a podcast where I do Y and would love to sit down with you for an interview."* The first request will be perceived as fanmail, whereas the second comes across as respect from a peer.

How it should be in your mind isn't necessarily the way it actually is. We would think everyone is equal, which may be true from a rights standpoint, but remember the currency of influence. The person or platform with more attention, credibility, and influence, is in the power position and is at the liberty to approve or deny your requests.

When pitching, assume a stance that is close to or at their level. Never say *"I'm your biggest fan"* or *"I've been following you for years."* Nothing of the sorts. Proceed to include some basic information about you, but no more than a paragraph. Approaching them as such does not sacrifice your credibility, nor does it come across as disingenuous, instead, you appear as if you're somebody *they should know*. The inverse is also true, and this approach may allow you to land an interview or feature on a platform that is in your mind *"out of your current reach."*

The worst that can happen is they say no or don't respond, and you can always follow up in 6 months to a year as your successes grow. Work so your previous mentors become the people you talk to within your network and your idols, the contacts in your phone. Credibility is built through the consistent exchange of influence through forms of edification.

Outside of these interactions, it is also built through the execution of actions that demand attention. This can be found in forms of: *publishing a book on industry subject matters, developing programs, building a business, making investments, writing contributor articles,* etc. Bring awareness to your accomplishments, not to flaunt, but in a way that demonstrates respect and balanced pride.

Announcements that start with the phrase *(or a variation of),* usually work well: *"I am proud to announce..."* Then proceed to talk about why it's important to you, if there's emotional significance, and what's coming next. Consider writing a press release for promotion and recording a video to pair with your written copy.

A: Start to get on the radar of journalists and media professionals who contribute to the outlets you want to be featured in. Narrow your search down by following those who write specifically about your profession. Get into their ecosystem, sign up for their email list, etc; and begin looking for source requests.

5.5 | Risk Management

If you decide to go skydiving, safety measures are put in place to ensure you are able to land properly and aren't freefalling to your death from 10,000 feet. It is the same with managing risks within your personal branding strategy. I've already talked about some of the risks that can manifest in pay-to-win press and botting your social media accounts, but what about cussing on camera or cracking a politically insensitive joke? How about running an ad campaign just to see no correlative ROI? Determining your risk tolerance requires you to factor in all aspects of your personal brand and identify what you want to be associated with and what you want to avoid.

The minister probably shouldn't cuss on camera, the politician may avoid the joke, and the person starting out would likely benefit more from organically growing their personal brand than throwing money around trying to go viral.

Risk management comes in the form of legal red tape, the lovely and painstaking part of hitting it big. This is by no means legal advice, nevertheless, these are some of the various steps I have implemented for my personal brand to enhance my security.

1. **Proper   Disclosures   and   Adherence:**
Adhering to local laws such as but not limited
to: *Affiliate Disclosures, Refund Policies, and
Privacy Policies.*

2. **Contracts:** Contracts for parties you are
representing or being represented by. My
booking agent and I have a contract. This is
not because there's any lapse of trust;
instead, as an act of good faith and as a fail
safe. If someone says you don't need a
contract, do another evaluation to ensure
their intentions are of pure heart as contracts
are meant to protect everyone involved.

3. **Non-disclosure Agreements:** When you're
working on a big project, have Intellectual
Property coming out, or are sharing trade
secrets, don't be afraid to ask the other party
to sign an NDA. Superstars have NDAs for
things as simple as attending parties and
events. It's a good way to express the gravity
of what you'd be discussing and set a
boundary for that relationship. NDAs also
create the perception that you are someone

who's working on something worth protecting.

4. **Researching In Advance:** Taking the time to educate yourself before you make a leap of faith is encouraged. From understanding the requirements to publishing a study, how to disclose the products you're advertising, or learning about the competitors to a potential investment.

5. **Documentation:** Saving important emails, text messages, and other forms of correspondence that can be used as evidence should a legal case ever rise, or if you need to launch a lawsuit for whatever reason.

Risk management does not exist to hinder you, but will act as your parachute, if God forbid, you are required to unwillingly jump out of the plane, or worse, the plane comes crashing down.

A: Evaluate the red tape you have for your personal brand and add more as needed.

5.6 | **Controversy With Purpose**

Whenever possible, it's best to avoid controversy that directly relates to your personal brand and reputation. Nonetheless, external controversies can be capitalized upon. Political commentators are an example of people who use current issues to create content that expresses their personal opinions and grow their brands. I am not suggesting you show your support for every new cause or go out of your way to leech off of drama, but seeing things for how they are compared to what they should be, can and when done correctly, result in well-timed *"chess moves."*

Is there a certain way services are handled in your profession that could be improved upon or viewed as unethical and can you provide genuine insights on the matter? As you see fit, be a *person of the people* and provide level-headed takes as somebody with insider experience.

If you do choose to comment on things outside of your trade such as politics, religion, or societal issues, do so with class and intention. You can build rapport with your network by expressing your broader opinions, yet, turn others away who do not agree. Avoid *"line in the sand"* moments that put you at odds with whole groups as reason is excluded when emotions become involved.

In recent political cycles, most notably presidential elections, it's become all too common to see people make explosive statements demeaning the character of another. It isn't limited to the United States as other countries are enduring similar challenges. Anybody with a platform seems to be saying that by supporting one candidate you're a fascist or racist, meanwhile the opposition claims that they're communistic and proceed to cast slurs. There is no value in doing this for your personal brand. **Controversy with no intent merely creates rage bait.** Newspapers and other media channels such as radio and television may thrive off of such headlines, quick cover stories, and gossip, but your personal brand does not.

My vendetta against scammers is a representation of controversy with purpose. I educate people in my audience on what to look out for, provide justifications as to why it's wrong, and then I swoop in from a point of authority and share what to do instead. *Educate, Justify, Prove*. It is controversial for me to go after another *"professional,"* but in doing so I am increasing my own credibility and validating my expertise. The alternative methods I provide might not be as sexy in terms of immediate payoffs, but they are much better in terms of *Sustainability [8]*.

My audience knows that I have a moral compass and fall underneath the ethicality of our society and that I genuinely want what is best for others. I recently posted that if you're paying to speak on stage, it means that your quality isn't on par to get paid, or at least not yet. I then interacted with the people who commented on my post and presented step-by-step solutions to becoming a paid speaker. I often make cut and dry posts such as this to form a *Content Loop*. A Content Loop is when you use past ideas to lay the foundation for future content. The initial post sparks interest whereas the next post expands on the idea. By diving into the reasons why paying to speak on stage is not a suitable option, I leaned into the market flaw, positioned myself as the expert, and validated my positioning with alternatives.

Early on, I would not recommend using or integrating controversy with purpose in your personal brand strategy, but once you get a footing and understand what you want your personal brand to represent, you can slowly integrate it into your arsenal.

1. *Highlight the flaw or headline.*
2. *Position yourself as the expert.*
3. *Provide information and clarification.*
4. *Justify and validate your perspective.*

Q: What is an example of someone in your profession who has utilized controversy to drive awareness for their personal brand? What takeaways can you deduce?

5.7 | **Destroying Credibility**

The destruction of credibility does not usually come from a single heinous action, rather the accumulation of lapses in judgment and poor decisions over an extended duration of time. Well-known directors and producers in Hollywood didn't destroy their reputations when stories of their sexual escapades were publicized. *They destroyed their reputations the moment they decided to use sex as opportunity cost.*

The marriage counselor who has a mistress should not be talking about their sexual enterprises, but more importantly, the marriage counselor should not have a mistress at all.

Sexual Energy is at the forefront of civilization. It's what creates your personal brand and is ironically the one thing that can do the most harm to it. It's where great men fall, good women get abused, and mistakes get made. *Sex is the act that produces man, and without procreation there wouldn't be any such thing as personal branding.* Many religious texts from the Bible to the Quran talk about the subject of sex at length and provide historical examples in their Theologies where sex triggered the downfall of remarkable people.

King David's reputation started with the death of Goliath and continued to grow until he became one of the greatest Kings of Jerusalem, yet, it was when he fell into temptation his blessings were challenged. According to the Christian Biblical text *(2 Samuel Chs. 11-12 and 1 Kings Chs. 1-2)* it was prophesied that his family would fall victim to the sword because of his lust and adultery with Bathsheba. His desire went so far as having her husband killed in a cover-up that you would expect to find in accounts from Niccolo Machiavelli's *The Prince*.

The destruction of your credibility does not usually have permanence unless you do something so egregious that there's no coming back from it. These acts are of the most awful type, such as extortion, murder and rape. Under most circumstances, it is possible to redevelop the trust that surrounds you but every situation has nuance. Jordan Belfort known synonymously as The Wolf of Wall Street wrote a book about his life and less than outstanding track record leading up to his repentance, that was later adapted into a Blockbuster movie where he was portrayed by one of the world's most famous actors.

You might be able to develop a holistically new audience that does not know of your history, but regardless of which path you take, what happened leading up to the destruction of your credibility will always find a way to come back to haunt you.

No degree of good press or how much you pay a public relations firm to squash stories, will be able to fully cover it up, at least *not in the age of the internet*. As your personal brand ascends to new heights, others will look to target you to achieve their private ambitions. You are now the controversy that other people are using to build their own platforms so take care to ensure your actions moving forward do not drive you towards reputational crises and learn to govern over what has happened in your past.

The destruction of your credibility may not appear in one fell swoop. The Roman Empire did not collapse overnight; it was through a series of wars, conquests, bad Emperors and political espionage that Rome eventually eroded. I remember seeing a post somebody wrote about a public speaker and in it, they went on to describe how he acted at the post-event dinner. He showed up late and was high, off of what, I do not know. How he behaved in private did not match his public persona. That story sticks with me to this day and I cannot look at him the same way. Now imagine that he did that after every event for the next year. His actions would become habitual and eventually destroy his credibility.

You can also harm your credibility insomuch as you can strengthen it by whom you associate yourself with. We have all heard the phrase *"You are the sum of the five people you spend the most time around."* Every time you're out in public and take a photo with somebody you meet, you are now associated with them forever. There are public figures to this day that are suffering the consequences of a photo they took with other powerful members of society 20 years ago who, in the last couple of years, were discovered to be some of the worst people society could ever possibly produce. A photo is not indicative of wrongdoing but that does not prevent people from thinking that you are a questionable character.

When it comes to the handling of perceptions, *"what should be"* versus *"what actually is,"* is inconsequential, it is what is perceived that counts. The lawyer who represents a murderer in a trial, will forever be known as the criminals' attorney. I remember a story my mom shared in my youth about how she was interested in practicing law until a public case of a man who supposedly killed his ex-wife, was acquitted. My mom decided that she could not be in an industry where she, as an attorney, could know someone did wrong but would be fighting to get them off the hook.

I am not suggesting that you must run a background check or hire a private investigator to look into every single person you come across, but if you have a gut feeling or hold previous information, exercise caution in how close of a relationship you build with them.

Q: Is there anything that you are currently doing or have recently done that, if surfaced, could harm your credibility and damage the public's perception of your personal brand? This is a good time to stop said action/s. Imagine if it did come to light; how would it make you feel, how would those closest to you be impacted, and how could you mitigate damage done?

5.8 | **Handling Defamation**

A difference exists between openly criticizing or questioning a person and purposely going out of your way to harm their reputation and good standing with the public. Trying to define the exact definition of defamation is challenging as it varies based on who you ask, the court system in place based on where you live, and various cultural differences. It is generally accepted that *defamation is the intentional spreading of rumors, words, and other things pertaining to a person or business that results in negative outcomes such as but not limited to, financial losses, lost opportunities, and unjust damages to one's reputation.*

In the United States everybody has the freedom of speech but when that person knowingly spreads a lie or is deceitful in the rumors they start *(ignorance included),* they could very well be held liable for a defamation lawsuit. When you're just starting out, defamation is unlikely to take place. Your old friends or family members might talk sarcastically about you behind your back, but they are not defaming you; they're expressing opinions and it's not as if they're going to have a major impact on your prospective success.

Let's say that there is a young adult woman in her mid-twenties who is an up-and-coming real estate agent under a local Realty Group. She's working to make a name for herself, creating content talking about her profession, highlighting a day in her life, and sharing profits. She has a good thing going, that is until one day she wakes up to see a rumor from a competing real estate agent saying that in order to close deals, she is selling her body and that her sex appeal is the only reason the market is coming to her.

For additional context, the realtor who started that rumor has been around for decades, is one of the top producers in their office, has a network of prestigious clients, and has sway in local politics. Without any evidence, he started a rumor to affect her business and well-being. Whatever his intentions were, to snuff out some of the competition, close more deals, or something else entirely, there is not a proper reason under the sun for him to ever have behaved that way. *This is in fact, defamation.*

The outcome of defamation is challenging to measure as there is no reliable way to identify who chose not to work with her based on a rumor or something they saw. Since building your personal brand and in this case real estate business brand, is more intricate and is a compilation of various marketing efforts and external factors, she would be unable to say *"I lost 10 houses because of this rumor."* If someone directly came to the agent and said *"I chose not to work with you as my real estate agent because of this information,"* then there is a more measurable case and evidence that she could present, with testimony, in the situation that she pursued legal action.

How do you begin to even handle a scenario as delicate as this? *Get a lawyer.* Inevitably, a lawyer will evaluate your current situation and determine if there is a realistic approach to filing litigation in court. Prior to this, they will no doubt issue a cease and desist letter that threatens further legal action if those statements are not rescinded. This does escalate the situation but you would be doing so with an appropriately strong party on your side.

You could alternatively approach the person who made those claims and try to find out their intentions, but would they likely take the time to discuss things? Not only that, it could escalate the situation and a positive outcome is improbable at best. It could also be dangerous especially as your fame grows, as the person may veer along the lines of an obsessive stalker who wants to get your attention.

The third option is to publicly address the claims. If you're just starting out there won't be a need to issue a press release, however, if you're farther along and have corporate clients, you might consider distributing one via your website, email list or in extreme cases, by newswire. You should take the time to craft a genuine social media post that presents your side of the story. The downside to publicly addressing the claims is that it will bring added awareness to a situation which some people might not even be aware of. Conversely, it might backfire on the scummy agent who started the rumors, as the people who are associated with you will perceive them to be a low life who nobody should do business with. *Be cautious in mentioning the individual by name.*

Defamation is not a fun game to play. Several years ago, I found myself in a situation where a disgruntled client that didn't perform any of the tasks I assigned to him, went on to harass myself, my significant other, and my associates. It got so bad I implemented the exact steps I highlighted in this subchapter and had my lawyer issue a cease and desist letter. I was prepared to file a defamation lawsuit and went as far as threatening to press criminal misdemeanor charges for harassment. To this day I have not heard from him. *If you are aiming to position yourself and become a high authority public figure, be prepared to start playing public figure games.*

Defamation can be found in two major forms, both of which have lasting impacts in their own right and when not taken care of, can spread and do serious harm to a person's reputation. *Libel* is defamation that comes in the form of written and published statements. These could be smear pieces on blogs, mass emails, social media posts, or talking negatively about a person in a book. What makes libel particularly dangerous and equally effective is the ability to spread through major distribution channels. People who already command influence who engage in libelous and defamatory behavior are playing with fire for if one post goes viral or their content gets shared between hundreds or even thousands of people, the damage can be everlasting and induce a tremendous challenge legally speaking. It may very well create an uphill battle for the person the statement was made about and the victim will be required to spend a significant portion of their time doing damage control and even then, the damage may be irreversible.

The press and media are somewhat immune to being accused of libel as their intent is not, *or rather should not be,* done in such a way meant to harm. Their role is to report facts to the general public. A news station that covers the controversy of a local politician is not aiming to ruin that politician's chances of getting elected, but are presenting pieces of evidence that they themselves have acquired. If there was an individual news anchor who had a vendetta against a politician this might be a different story, but even then talking about defamation in reference to politics is unconventional as politicians are supposed to be under close examination. It amazes me how some people want to become President of the United States when the highest office in the land requires such a degree of transparency and snooping into their background that nothing remains hidden.

The second form of defamation, *Slander*, is spoken. These could be private conversations, public statements in voice chat rooms, or somebody going on a talk show and spreading hurtful rumors. In 2024 there was a hundred-million dollar defamation lawsuit filed between a public real estate mogul and a former Chief Executive Officer of a very large corporation. This CEO stated in a social audio application that the mogul was effectively a scammer and a *"false billionaire."* This led to a massive legal battle and presumably tens of thousands of dollars in legal fees and a months-long skirmish between the two. To my knowledge, it was eventually settled, but the damage was done due to the amount of influence that the former CEO held. Whether it was true or not true, again, does not matter.

Defamation is nasty for everybody involved and it is much better to avoid making any negative statements about others especially when you don't have the facts or are operating emotionally. Avoid *name-dropping* or mentioning anybody by name as it makes you appear to be a person who thrives on drama and as though you are targeting others for their success, especially if they are within your profession. Avoid situations that could cause further investigation into areas of your life you would prefer to keep private.

T: Research various defamation cases between individuals. What circumstances led to the cases being filed and what statements were made?

5.9 | Dealing with Crises

A crisis is defined as *a negative spotlight on something that happened to you, something you did,* or *someone you are associated with that is less than favorable.* The process of dealing with crises shares many parallels with what we discussed in *Leaning Tower [5.1].* There are several options made available to you depending on the situation such as:

1. **Apathy:** Acting as if the crisis at hand does not exist and not taking any blame whatsoever. This doctrine believes, *"The less awareness, the better."*

2. **Claim Ignorance:** You did not know something was going on or that you were in the wrong. This action may stand on the line of deceit. Consider an employee with insider information about an upcoming launch. They then proceeded to make investments into their company or the related companies' stocks. When questioned, they could claim ignorance and act like they didn't know it was illegal insider trading.

3. **Addressing the Situation Head On:** My personal favorite as it is indicative of the most accountability. However, it is absolutely useless if you do not take the necessary steps to change and make sure that the crisis does not happen again. An example would be a person who cheats on their spouse, says they won't do it again, but returns to their exact behavior weeks later.

4. **Separation:** Separating yourself from the controversy altogether. This is when you bring in a public relations firm or agent to speak on your behalf and act as a mediator. Done poorly or if done at all, it can appear desperate and be perceived as an admission of guilt.

5. **Masquerading Through Charity:** Does doing good deeds right a wrong? Imagine you are the President of one of the world's largest oil companies. Unfortunately, an oil spill occurred and in order to save face you publicly address the disaster while simultaneously starting a non-profit campaign where the company donates

proceeds of profit to an environmental charity. This strategy, for rarely appearing genuine, at least provides some solace. There are events where charity isn't as impactful. A celebrity who is ousted as a raging abusive alcoholic can't turn around and start donating to charities that support addiction to look like a saint.

Not every crisis is the same and before you make any sudden movements you might come to regret, evaluate your current situation and map out an action plan. Should you fall into a crisis, like accidentally doing business with a scammer, being at an event where one of the speakers is ousted, or other mistakes of your own making, crises are very rarely the end of the world. Addressing the controversy oftentimes lead to the early fledglings of resolution.

Building your personal brand is an endeavor of a lifetime and it is only a matter of time for something to happen that is less than ideal. You could even view a crisis as indicative that you're moving in the right direction...Please do not take that out of context. ***Do not seek crises.***

Acknowledging your mistakes does not make you any less of a person; acknowledging mistakes shows character and that you are willing to accept accountability and adopt change. It is then up to you to never make those mistakes again. Insanity is *doing the same thing multiple times expecting different results*. It is not up to you to do backwater testing and gamble with your reputation. Not all mistakes are equal and some are more significant than others, but the principles in how you respond to them usually share similarities.

Society appreciates transparency and if you act as if you are holier than thou, you're putting on a façade which only gets you so far. You should absolutely continue to position yourself as a public figure, but even Napoleon Bonaparte foolishly marched into Russia. If you wanted to take it a step further, you could turn your mistake into a public learning lesson, and share your findings. Talk about your blunders and some of the decisions leading up to them, and conversely what you learned.

One of the reasons you are reading my book is so you do not have to make the same personal branding mistakes or learn this all from scratch. This is preferable as you are able to cut time frames and move with more speed when compared to your peers.

Don't expect everybody to respect or feel a sense of vindication with your acknowledgment of mistakes. You're not going to have a complete satisfaction rate, but you are mitigating and minimizing any long-term damage that occurs to your personal brand. Acting as the perfect narcissist who neglects accountability is not something you would like to be known for.

Q: Have you ever dealt with a public crisis? What led to the situation's escalation and what resolution did you reach?

5.10 | **Manipulation**

As your influence grows and more people know about you, trust you, and believe in what you're building and pursuing, you are given a tremendous privilege and a gift. This privilege is a simultaneous burden that requires you to hold yourself to a higher standard when compared to the average person. You're given the opportunity to command change and influence others so much so I would dare say personal branding creates the closest thing to the *Midas Touch*. This gift is manipulative when misused with the wrong intent. I am not advocating for manipulation in any sense of the word, but I'd like to bring awareness to this exceptional power.

Manipulation can be defined as *an abuse of a position of authority*. The executive who is capable of getting their employees to do whatever they please in hopes of a promotion. The marketer who gets people to make investments into things they know carry no true value. The celebrity who manipulates narratives at their will during political campaigns in exchange for financial compensation. As your credibility and reach grows, *your ability to manipulate grows in parallel.*

In Nicollo Machiavelli's *The Prince*, he shares the story of Cesare Borgia and Remirro de Orco. Borgia had Orco act as his pawn to create order and get their citizens in line. His methods were less than humane, often perceived as harsh. After the intended goal of order was met, Duke Borgia distanced himself from Orco, claimed ignorance and had his general executed in the public square by the townspeople. This is one of the greatest examples I could provide on manipulation as it shows a person of great power abusing their position to fabricate a preferential outcome, synchronously securing their own office.

Directed influence of any sort is manipulation. The distinction is found in the intent behind the action itself. If a public figure knowingly engages in a behavior that is wrong, it's manipulation of the worst kind, whereas if it's done out of ignorance or good faith such as the endorsement of a cause a person genuinely cares about and wants to see do well, the circumstances surrounding it are different. Influence is the heat you are looking for but if you don't employ proper safety-precautions and respect its dangers, you will get burned.

T: Write out a personal Code of Conduct. What do you stand for and what morals and ethics will you adhere to in building your personal brand?

5.11 | **Giving Endorsements**

In time, you will be asked to offer endorsements. Whether that be to promote a product, write a review, record a testimonial, or speak on the qualities of another person, exercise caution before attaching yourself to another entity; recall the subchapter on *Destroying Credibility [5.7]*. Your followers have expectations and endorsements are extensions of your good faith and your personal influence.

Make it your second nature to do research prior to giving an endorsement of any kind. When endorsing a company, product or a service look into the people who developed it and those who already promote it. Understand its history and have a conversation with the team if possible. As for endorsing another person or professional, evaluate the narrative that surrounds them, what they stand for, your experiences with them, and the intent behind why they're requesting said endorsement.

Due to external variables, if you do make an endorsement you come to regret, it is possible to withdraw it, but you may lose credibility in doing so. There will be those who listened to you and already bought or started supporting the entity you endorsed. If done without proper class and emotional awareness, your withdrawal will present you as someone simply chasing a check. To help avoid this, supplement your personal brand with other ways of generating revenue to communicate that you are not reliant on that source of income.

The entire model of influencer marketing is built around endorsements. Influencers are telling their communities to make decisions based on association. They mention particular perks and services, but the need is not always what drives people to buy or support, it is their seal of approval. *Withdrawing requires you to explain why.* If you just say *"I no longer endorse or support xyz,"* It's distasteful and indicative that you have something to hide or do not believe the tribe you've built deserves your explanation.

Providing substantial reasoning validates your good standing. An example of this would be endorsing a brand only to find out their products are unethically sourced or are arbitraged and illegitimate. An avoidable mistake, yes, but you're bound to make them from time to time with your personal brand. Do your due diligence first.

On a personal front, *Edification* is the endorsement of an individual. Essentially, it is when somebody offers supportive statements about another's accomplishments, character, and overall being. *It is an exchange of influence,* the most valuable currency the world has to offer. Exchanging influence is *credibility by association,* as opposed to *guilty by association.* Many professionals use edification as one of their most potent sales tools. When a car salesman walks the lot with a buyer, their manager may approach them and sing praises about the associate's attention to detail and prowess. In doing so, the buyer may feel more confident, knowing that their *"guide"* is well-regarded.

When a person shares a piece of your content online they are edifying you and are associating your content with their domain. *Never edify without properly vetting and verifying that the person is worthy of edification.* You can do so by talking about your authentic experiences with them, how you've seen them perform, and so on, but speak from a place of honesty.

The only way that you can become a true figure of public interest is through the edification of enough people. Anyone can call themself an expert but that is biased. If you can get other people to call you an expert and talk about why they support you *(without asking),* you are in an opportune position.

It is a position that holds power and reflects support from the market. In turn, your position lowers the objection threshold and resolves any potential concerns others might have.

Today public figures can go from 100,000 followers to 1,000,000 easier than it is to go from 100 to 1,000, because in the mind of the consumer, somebody who has 100,000 followers has already been validated. You may gain new followers simply because they do not want to miss out on *the next big thing*. That fear of missing out *(FOMO)* drives us into the herd mentality or groupthink.

As a final rule, it is always better to give endorsements without being asked. This is a sign of good faith and lowers the potential risk of manipulated intent.

T: Research recent celebrity endorsement campaigns. Did the celebrity actually use the product or service or was it simply a payday?

5.12 | **Audience Fatigue**

Offering too many endorsements and promoting too many things dilutes your personal brand's value and can fatigue your audience. *Be selective with* _what_ *and* _how_ *you promote.* Pushing a new promotion everyday is not as effective as promoting a few quality offers per month. There must be a balance between selfless value and selfish aggrandizing. Trying to get your network to do something for days or weeks on end is a surefire way of inciting *Audience Fatigue.* Where did the *"authentic"* you go? In this example of audience fatigue, your character gets put into question; being perceived as a sellout is the last thing you'd want.

The other form of fatigue occurs over time and manifests in a lapse in inspiration. You can only use the same material so many times before it gets old. I do believe from time to time you should continue promoting old content, as the creative process is the most challenging and usually deserves more exposure, but only do so if you plan on promoting something new soon after. An artist can get people to listen to a song they distributed three years ago, but are keeping their fans engaged with the hopes that new music is also on the horizon.

The final form of audience fatigue is found when your network runs dry. Relationships require effort so if you choose to be reclusive and not talk to anybody, do not be surprised when your network is not growing or if opportunities stop coming your way. The time leading up to publishing this book, I barely spoke to anybody to such a point I had people reaching out to see if I had died. That is nobody's fault but my own. Adopting *The Power of 3* *[6.5]* as covered in the next chapter *Marketing [6]*, is an easy strategy you'll come to appreciate and implement.

Why does audience fatigue happen?

Simply put, *ego*.

Whether you think you're King Midas himself and can promote nonstop or that you're too big to continue doing the actions that led you to your current achievements, your ego is the cause, and exhaustion is the aftermath. Keep your ego in check and benefits will continue to present themselves.

While ego can potentially be your greatest downfall, it can also be your greatest asset. Without it, you will lack the confidence required to encourage your audience and set an example worth following. Provide as much tactical advice and value as possible in your content and efforts. You could tell someone to get motivated, or you could provide the exact steps that you use to *stay motivated*. You could talk about why everyone should build their personal brand or you could provide the exact blueprint.

Let your community know that you appreciate them and on occasion express your gratitude. Consider offering a quick word of advice when you feel drawn to do so. Honor your supporters in public and in private as showing gratitude is a sign of leadership; humility is visible in the person who shares in their accomplishments. The idea of being humble should not be something that imprisons a person or prevents them from pursuing their goals out of the fear that they will be prideful or *"better than thou."*

From a psychological standpoint, communicating your gratitude deepens the resonance between you and the other person. *It is a point of connection that establishes rapport.* In a world full of narcissists, be a grateful friend.

As your personal brand scales in sheer volume, *Groupthink* might take over. Groupthink is when a metaphorical second mind forms and is why consumers play off of one another in their criticisms, complain about their shared experiences, and dwell on points of contention. Entire ecosystems are developed within the comment sections of social media posts because of groupthink.

You are at the pinnacle of a mountain others aspire to climb and just as you once looked up to others, others are now looking up at you. This past year I came to the realization that where I am today, younger me wanted to be. Now imagine you take that feeling and market it to the masses. You can set the example and will forever be the person who got another to take massive action. The mentors I vehemently learned from and presently acknowledge will forever be held in high regard in my mind because of the impact and influence they had on me.

You can be that person to another.

A: Once a month or as you see fit, make a post expressing gratitude for everyone who supports you. This takes 30 seconds to do but will have an immeasurable impact on your personal brand.

5.13 | **Giving Your Word**

"Your word is your bond." — A cliché which rings true, especially for your personal brand and individual reputation. If you say that you're going to do something, for your sake, do it! In our age of fast-paced competition and instant results, people will move on quickly, especially if you haven't had the time to build rapport.

Think about situations from your past when you broke your word; it doesn't matter if it was intentional or accidental, *how did it make you feel?* More importantly, *how did the other person respond?* A person whose word isn't backed up by actions does not foster an attitude of trust or communicate competence. We can have a separate discussion altogether about keeping your word to yourself, but I digress. I want your focus to be entirely on managing and directing the proper perceptions in the minds of those you interact with. If you say that you'll be somewhere at a specific time, be there. Whether you're being flown out for an event, selling a product or service, or are getting hired for a job, it's all under the pretense that you'll deliver.

Giving Your Word is also how you become more sought after. Imagine having a reputation for being the professional known for moving mountains with their voice and who can open doors of opportunity using their network. I would be much more comfortable edifying or endorsing someone who has always remained true to their word than the person I have to follow up with to see an otherwise expected result.

If there is a moment in time where you must go back on your word, follow the same steps as highlighted for withdrawing endorsements [5.11]. Address the reason why you are breaking your word and work to minimize repercussions. Explanations are almost always deserved but how detailed you would like to be in your explanation is up to you. Understand that breaking your word may result in broken relationships as you can only go back on your bond so many times before good faith runs dry.

Q: Is your word always good? If you answered no, take a look at situations where you've broken your word. When was the last time you talked to that person? This may be a good time to reach out and apologize.

5.14 | **Compiling Wins**

One of my flaws is my incapability to deeply appreciate wins. As my personal brand has grown throughout the last decade I have had to manually force myself to stop and take note of what it is I have accomplished. It is the nature of individuals with ambition to focus on what they're doing instead of basking in what they've already done or where they've been. From a mindset perspective, I'm not here to tell you that one way is better than the other as I am still figuring that part out, but there is truth in saying that by *Compiling Wins,* future successes become easier to obtain. *Larger opportunities seek out positive track records.*

It may require pitching 200 people to come on their show to land your first 20 to 30 interviews, but once your record is established and you have an *In-The-Media Sheet* and thoroughly developed *Media Kit,* your appearances begin to speak for you. Other professionals can listen to them to gauge your degree of expertise. There will eventually be less *convincing* and more time spent narrowing down what you *choose* to do; the greater the public figure, the more selective the actions.

Top performers, industry aside, may not agree to come on a student's show or sit down with middle-aged men recording a podcast from their garage. Is this a proper expenditure of their energy? Limited-visibility opportunities are less attractive than those that are more on par with their current reputation. This is but one scenario of how compiling wins can be used to one's advantage.

Take the consultant who is armed with client case studies. A case study under this context is a collection of information that verifies results, i.e, *before and after examples, generated revenue or clicks,* and *direct testimonials.* If there is a choice between the consultant who might charge a lower rate but doesn't have any case studies and the consultant who charges more but has verifiable and satisfactory gains, who do you think would be able to land more business? A professional isn't going to start by charging $1,000 for one consultation. I only charged $20 for my first call. Eventually, I raised my rate from $20 to $500, $500 to $1,000 and so on, but it took numerous conversations, consultations, and substantiated results for me to feel comfortable doing so.

A fashion designer starts with one or two designs before they can ever launch a full fashion line or partner with luxury brands. Compiling wins is about directing attention so that a partnership is perceived as undeniably beneficial. What have you done so far via your personal brand that you can tell others about? What awards, certifications, and milestones could you promote? This is not meant to be approached in a braggadocious way, fiending for attention, but as subtle statement pieces that provide evidence to your ambitions.

When treated seriously enough for longer than a few years, your personal brand is attributed with authority. Others will have heard about your name before they ever have a conversation with you or click *"follow."* This is when your audience works in your favor and serves as your best marketers. Word of mouth being as powerful as it is, requires context and the more wins a public figure has, the higher the likelihood wins continue in influx.

A business that has hundreds of positive reviews not only stands out amongst its competitors, but a psychological anomaly occurs where people will be more likely to write reviews of their own. There is a sense of ownership in the establishment's accomplishments. A customer couldn't care less about becoming a public figure yet enjoys feeling validated in leaving a review.

Relationships are a form of capital. *Relationship capital* acts as a sort of bank; when you do things for others, you are putting capital into that relationship just like you compile other tangible wins. When you need help or have a favor to ask, you're taking a withdrawal so ensure that you are depositing more than you are withdrawing.

As a species, we like winning and enjoy associating with winners. From a primal point of view, it makes us more attractive and introduces added comfort to our existence; inversely, compile enough failures and you may just turn into a court jester.

T: List as many wins from your last 12 months as possible; these should be both about personal and professional successes. At the end of this exercise reflect on how you feel and determine the wins you'd like to drive more awareness to.

| 6 |

Marketing

Steps to reach more people and expand your personal brand's awareness

6.1 | Marketing Essentials

I will forever believe in the importance of spending some extra time on developing your *Elevator Pitch [4.3]* and brand messaging before you go out to market. *I am by no means encouraging you to make an excuse for not marketing.* If you spend a couple of weeks working on this, then great, but overthinking can and will harm your prospective returns.

There are literally thousands of ways to market yourself. Your personal brand is you, so this should not come with difficulty. Gamify what you are doing and make it enjoyable. View strengthening your personal brand as a game where the end goal is hitting unprecedented levels. So many stop before they can enjoy the fruits of their labor, yet marketing can be as simple as having a conversation while you're waiting to be seated at a restaurant or boarding a flight in the airport. Look around you; everyone is operating on autopilot, but if you can break that trend and adopt the old world method of talking to strangers, you'll find your friendships growing and relationships advancing.

Anytime you shake a person's hand and introduce yourself, you are engaging in a form of marketing. From ordering your morning cup of coffee and exchanging information with the barista, to attending networking events and appearing on major platforms. When networking, always be the one who holds the contact information as most will not reach back out. If you're telling the person your social media or giving out your phone number, ask to hold their phone and put it in directly or have a NFC *(Near Field Communication)* business card. This technology allows them to directly scan your contact information. As your authority scales and you become more out of reach, you'll notice the opposite happens and more people will go out of their way to talk to you.

Each form of marketing has its purpose. By reverse engineering other brands and personal brands you can, to a degree, begin to understand what marketing tactics deserve most of your time. Certain tactics may generate results faster, whereas others may be prolonged. At first glance, the return may appear small, but will be greater in the long-term. You'll generate a keen sense of what is the most effective and what isn't, and the ability to decipher trends in the market before they take off. You'll understand what you enjoy and what comes naturally. This can't be taught nearly to the same degree as it can be learned hence I'd encourage you to experiment and try out new things. Do not refrain from taking action over the fear of failure, for if you do, how can you anticipate ever developing the skill?

In marketing, there is no such thing as failure unless your tactic is outright egregious and generates near irreversible and negative public relations. Otherwise, you simply have tactics that are more powerful than others. Take what you can from the experience, learn from it, and apply it in an adapted form later on.

I'd like to briefly discuss an additional tactic, known as *Guerrilla Marketing*. This is an unconventional way of getting your message out there such as the Chick-Fil-A cows on billboards; I remember growing up seeing the faux cows painting their misspelled marketing message *"Eat Mor Chikin."* Leverage your surroundings to your benefit. There was once a time where I left business cards in the self-development section of a well-visited bookstore in *The Grove,* a popular shopping mall of Los Angeles. A few weeks later I got a message from somebody who found my business card in the book they bought. Outside of the one message there wasn't any correlated ROI, but it was the mentality which I developed that made it worth it. Guerrilla Marketing won't be a strategy most personal brands adopt.

The contemporary artist could go out nude in public, covered in paint to generate buzz for their new gallery and the musician may choose to partner with a fast food chain for an exclusive meal. Your energy is better spent on campaigns which have direct and measurable benefits; that is until you get to the stage of scaling a team exclusively for your personal brand. It's not like a person starting out is able to record a video in the back of their car and spend millions of dollars to run a Superbowl Ad.

T: List off as many marketing methods as possible. Which one/s appeal to you and which ones do you think will be the most beneficial to your personal brand?

6.2 | **Optimization and Consolidation**

It is impossible to portray the full extent of your character and interests in one marketing message so when crafting the phrase which is front and center in your *Elevator Pitch [4.3]*, in your biographies, and other materials, it comes down to prioritization. Including a personal hook with a professional punchline is what I've found to be the most functional in terms of establishing early stages of rapport and communicating competency.

My current phrase is *"Addicted to coffee and standards. I help emerging and established public figures optimize and scale their personal brands."* When I do not have space due to platform character limits, I'll shorten it to say *"Addicted to coffee. I help public figures optimize and scale their personal brands."* The core of the message remains untouched—*Seamless Branding [4.16]*.

When promoting new releases or offers, don't focus on telling the entire story, but on the information required to hook someone. Once they're figuratively *"caught"* it's up to you to share information that is relative to them. When you sign contracts, you rarely read all of the fine print, but what do you pay attention to? The key terms and benefits. When pitching a journalist for a press feature, it's not about convincing them and sending slews of information. The journalist will read the subject and the first few lines of text most pertinent to their story. If they want or need more from you, they'll ask, or, in the best cases, will rely on your public image to verify your claimed expertise.

Your personal brand is your resumé on steroids. Displaying your credentials and filling out as many text fields as possible answers more questions than it creates.

The stories you told years ago will not be the same stories you continue to tell. Today I refrain from sharing all of the details from my childhood unless I'm aiming to substantially connect on an emotional level. Instead, I choose to talk about the information pertinent to strategy and tactical value. A news segment for example, is limited on time and if you spend the majority of it reminiscing, you'll miss out on the opportunity to position yourself as the expert on the subject matter; *this is optimization.*

In reference to *Consolidation*, get good at highlighting germane aspects of your story and compressing time frames. How can you tie coming from a single-parent household to your later career choices? Did it impact you in an important way? If you were involved in sports as a child what lessons have helped you in your career? Are these aspects of your life you want publicly known or to be associated with?

Luxury brands emphasize experiences more than they do features. They'll talk about how you feel driving that car or wearing that watch. The craftsmanship is expected as it backs up their prestige. If you are known for delivering a speech in a certain style, you'll naturally share the stories that led you to becoming a speaker. Stories alone don't matter nearly as much as what those stories produce. *Emotions.*

A lot of what is covered under marketing, concerns the rewards that come from a maturing personal brand. You are letting your actions speak for you; remind yourself of your *Deliverables [4.11].*

T: Take an aerial view of your personal brand. Is it all over the place or organized? What can you optimize for length and impact?

6.3 | **Writing Your Marketing Message**

To write an effective marketing message, apply what I discussed in the previous subchapter on *Optimization and Consolidation [6.2]*. Now that you know that you need to have a personal hook with a professional punchline, what do you want people to know about you? Starting with a personable hook establishes rapport and conveys that you're more than just a professional. You're a human being. When I'm working with clients, I ask them about their passions, their interests, their hobbies, and what they could talk about for hours on end if given the opportunity.

The professional punchline is relatively self-explanatory and is ironically what I find easiest to create. Let's use the example of a graphic designer. They will need to communicate what they do, who they're working with, and throw in a synonym or two to express an elevated experience. Compare these marketing messages as a brief exercise.

"I design graphics for corporations."

"I design the graphics for the businesses you buy from."

The second message is clearly better, but it lacks an outcome.

"I design the graphics for the businesses you buy from, that give you confidence in your purchase."

Even then, it doesn't clearly define the kind of businesses that you work with.

"I make unique designs for product-based businesses that give their buyers confidence in their purchases."

That's better, but it's still missing emotion.

"I design unique product labels for the companies you buy from every day to make your home, feel like home."

This marketing message communicates that they are a designer who focuses on product marketing design for B2C businesses, offer one-of-a-kind designs, and incorporates a familial aspect into their work. If we combine this professional punchline with a personal hook we're really getting somewhere.

"I play more soccer than I watch. I design unique product labels for the companies you buy from every day to make your home, feel like home."

I would like for you to read that marketing message aloud several times. How does it make you feel? Now read that message without the personal hook. For something as simple as *"I play more soccer than I watch,"* without it, the material lacks personality in such a way that is almost inexplicable.

When I was recently asked what is *"too personal"* to show, I responded with the following:

"Decide what parts of your life you want to have associated with your public image. If you have children but for privacy concerns don't want them to appear with you in a front-facing manner, you won't want to create a marketing message that says 'Mother of 3 wonderful kids. (insert professional

punchline).' If you are a dedicated triathlete outside of your career, you could mention that aspect instead."

The point of including personal aspects with your personal brand is to build rapport and community. What you decide to show and hide is entirely up to you, but ask yourself *"What is my goal in including this?"*

The process I just took you through is similar to that in which I would take a client. If you can communicate *who you are, who you serve, what's special about you,* and more importantly, *attach emotional meaning to the outcome,* you will assuredly stand out from your competitors. It also attaches credibility to your claim. In my own marketing message, when I reference *"emerging and established public figures,"* it tells anyone who is reading my profile that I'm somewhat exclusive in who I serve. There is exclusivity in my client base which in turn, increases the perception a stranger has upon first glance.

Your marketing message is one of the first lines of defense for your personal brand and either produces a negative or positive first impression. It takes multiple tries to perfect your marketing message so that you truly fall in love with it. Even then, you will likely feel like it could be better and will spend the coming months *(or years)* transforming it. As your personal brand evolves, update your marketing message to reflect who you are today, not who you were five years ago.

T: Rewrite your marketing phrase until you find a combination that has both a personal hook and professional punchline that communicates your intended message.

6.4 | **Building Your Contact List**

As the saying goes, *your network is your net worth*. Growing a contact list of people and other professionals, whether in your industry or not, makes you invaluable to have around. A quality contact list allows you to solve problems with a simple introduction. You can approach conversations with tact and ask others about their pain points knowing that you are able to help. If they say they are struggling with content creation, introduce them to your recommended designer.

This falls under *Giving Endorsements [5.11]* so take into account our discussion on how and when to give them. Your seal of approval is a double edged sword and can cut in the perfect places. You will forever hold a place in their mind as the problem solver if your recommendation exceeds their expectations. This will result in them wanting to reciprocate that generosity *(Relationship Capital)*.

If you don't have an immediate need, gathering intelligence and meeting quality professionals decreases the amount of time you would need to otherwise spend if and when the need does arise. When I wanted to get a custom 1-of-1 soundtrack for my audio branding to be used in vlogs, at speeches, etc; instead of having to go out and search for someone, I reached out to Mitchel Hines, an extremely talented artist I already knew. We had a relationship built over several years and his quality was evident. I didn't have to ask around or waste any time trying to find the best person for the job.

If we flip the dynamic and approach the subject from an alternate point of view, you must position yourself as the go-to-expert within your space. Your name should be the first to come up in private conversations, as the easiest clients to close and the best opportunities come from formal introductions where you're edified.

Because of an introduction, I was able to land a paid speaking engagement with ease. It was coming off of the success at the Atlantic-Oase Professional Conference when I was CC'ed into an email chain by an industry leader. An email and phone call later the gig was booked, check in the mail. Without taking the time to have conversations, none of this would have been possible.

I'm not suggesting that you spend hours on end meeting with everyone you see, but taking 10 to 15 minutes for short introductions sharpens your people skills and grows your contacts. Having a contact list will make growing your email list easy as they will feel more comfortable handing over their private information and being a part of your ecosystem. *If you want more introductions, lean into your credentials and create peace of mind.*

Q: If your main marketing channels disappeared in some act of God or bankruptcy, would you have a contact list to fall back on? Is it suitable as it stands to continue generating results?

6.5 | **The Power of 3**

The Power of 3 is an easy marketing strategy that transcends technology and time. I first developed the strategy around 2019 as my clients increasingly struggled to find simple ways to grow their network. It calls for you to introduce yourself to 3 strangers every day for 90 days. After a month 90 new people will now know about you. Do this consistently for 90 days and that number grows to 270. Although this may not seem significant, something interesting happens when the 270 begin to tell their own networks about you. Imagine if all of these people told at least one person or shared a piece of your content. The number of connections would double to 540. If this happens again, it increases your reach to 1,080 and so on and so forth. *Compounding results in exponential growth.*

These numbers obviously represent a perfect scenario, but if you were to expand your efforts and commit to The Power of 3 for an entire year, by day 365, your network will have gone from 0 to 1,095; this does not factor in any potential compounding. 1,095 people can fill most hotel rooms, an entire section of a stadium, earn you a best-selling book, and put your podcast in the top 5% of shows.

Social media and the internet makes it easy to discount numbers that aren't in the millions, yet, when you are intentional with whom you decide to connect with, you could be building 3 new relationships with executives and decision-makers, investors and mentors, authors and journalists. The Power of 3 doesn't exist *just to compound*. It's intended to develop your mentality and lay the foundation needed to scale.

How you implement this strategy is entirely up to you. You can use social media, go out in person, or a combination thereof. Stop viewing everyone as a number and start viewing them as genuine connections and people who live lives of their own, have careers, interests, families, and passions.

A: Use the Power of 3 on a daily basis and make it a part of your personal branding habits *[8.7]*. Track your results weekly, monthly, quarterly, and yearly.

6.6 | **Communicating Intent**

It is natural for humans to have a degree of selfish intent behind their actions. Idealists make the argument that you should always be selfless and put others first, but we are not living in an idealistic world, are we? I am in the school of thought that there should be a balance between selfish intent and selfless giving. As you are building out your personal brand, you're making a conscious choice to make it about you.

Even if you're motivated by mission or philanthropy, you subconsciously know, and whether you accept this or not, that you will receive and reap the benefits of spearheading a movement. If you are a coach who earns a living off of helping others, you might claim that it is about those you are serving and the success stories you're garnering, but in private, you likely enjoy the way that it makes you feel. There is no such thing as pure selflessness unless we're referring to holy men themselves. Discussing the story which led you to becoming a mission-oriented individual allows others to join in on your journey and also support it.

The question now becomes *"How do you communicate your intent with these newfound relationships?"* Transparency returns your investment many times over and most appreciate it if you are up front with them. Connecting with somebody whose services you currently do not need initially appears fruitless until you tell them that by having the conversation you are looking for a partner you can refer clients to.

Communicating intent is the way that you salvage relationships and lay the framework for stronger ones to develop. It's the equivalent of having a contractor visit your house to give you a quote. Before you ever make the phone call, let them know that if the quote is reasonable you intend to get the work done and otherwise you might explore your options. This transparency may indirectly influence them to give you a more reasonable price and ensures that they do not feel like you are wasting their time.

Letting your intent be known to your public circle creates advocates out of your community. Since you now have the understanding that there must be a purpose in building your personal brand, share the _why_ and the _how_. For those solely motivated by vanity, it is not wise to say *I want to be famous just because,* but sharing that you're consciously contributing to your personal brand so you can generate business for your company will probably lead to more interest and sales.

Publicizing aspects of your plan and strategy demonstrates organization and casts a vision. Visionaries are appreciated more than the common man. The child who sets out to become a football superstar communicates their intent all throughout their childhood. Their parents are supportive of their journey because they know their child is working towards something great and will do anything to make that dream a reality. From purchasing the proper equipment, to helping them land a place on the team; if that child was quiet about their dreams, it would never manifest.

The student who graduates and enters Medical School communicates the intent that they want to become a doctor. Their professors, who understand that this student is serious, will go out of their way to ensure that they are set up to succeed.

Every great company sets forth a mission statement and a vision for what they are working towards. We have private companies with the ambition of going to Mars, companies working to become more environmentally friendly, product based companies and even car manufacturers, have set philanthropic goals at the front and center of every sale.

The nihilist would say that these are little more than marketing schemes to get more funding or attract more buyers. Regardless of the intention, the outcomes and vision remain. I'd encourage you to make a *public proclamation of vision.* I did this the first month of launching Mashman Consulting Group *(MCG)* when I said that by the year 2035 we would have 500 Consultants working for the company providing consulting services of their own, and that we would be the global Number 1 Personal Branding Firm. I have a decade to accomplish this goal but I wanted to let others know I was in this for the long haul.

Again, in the age of microwave meals, positioning yourself as a long-term thinker that prefers Crock-Pot meals is a strong competitive advantage. You don't have to talk about your vision on a daily basis but as you see fit; whether that be via an interview or an occasional piece of content, let people in on what you are pursuing. Use this as an opportunity to develop an accountability group, assemble a private circle, or even offer mentorship to somebody else who is early in their journey.

These are not selling opportunities, these are opportunities to develop a deeper connection with the people who will potentially know you for the rest of their lives. Celebrities remain relevant decades after their breakout and have stayed front and center in the minds of millions. They've all encountered turbulent times, but we don't focus on their failures, we focus on their successes.

Adopting this kind of thinking followed by immense action, validates your claims and positioning all the more.

T: Use this time to meditate on your true intent behind building your personal brand. Think about what you are looking to gain from others as well as what you're offering in exchange.

6.7 | **Incentives**

What incentives are you offering people for championing your personal brand? These are incentives other than *Education, Entertainment, Motivation/Inspiration,* and *Connection.* Enter entrepreneurial thinking. Businesses offer *Incentives* of many kinds such as customization, discounts, exclusive features, limited edition memorabilia, early access to new launches, and so on. Your personal brand should be doing the same.

Not only do incentives communicate authority and create the feeling of progression, they also motivate somebody to take action *now* rather than later. The incentives you choose to offer vary based on who you are and your industry. It may not make sense for the life insurance agent to offer an early access group for upcoming content or behind the scenes looks, meanwhile, the niched educator who talks about animals may greatly benefit from such a thing.

The journalist may not have an email list specifically for teaching people on how to pitch, however, they may use their email list as a chance to be *first in the know* for upcoming stories or give their subscribers an opportunity to pitch and be featured in said stories.

A great way to identify possible incentives would be to reverse engineer and attempt to measure what others in your space are doing. Consider how far along you are in your own personal brand and determine if it makes sense to launch such an opportunity now or later. Every idea that you have does not have to be executed straight away. Recognize the difference between pushing something off because you don't think that you are good enough or doing so because it makes strategic sense.

The person who just started making internet content and only has a couple followers should continue publicly posting until they develop a degree of advocacy. Then they can consider offering something more private as their fanbase develops with people who are coming back to consume their content.

Certain incentives also require an investment on your part, from paying for hosting, fees for registration and processing, or in the time to develop the designs and necessary materials. Such is the cost of doing business. Your incentives' return must be greater than the initial investment. Launching an email list may not provide an immediate ROI but in time will pay dividends; it puts your content directly in the pockets and inbox of every single person who is subscribed. You will eventually create an entire ecosystem of offerings for your personal brand.

Early on, this was one of my biggest mistakes as I wanted to chase so many new shiny objects and didn't have the discipline to consistently execute. To use the example of the email list, if your initial offering was daily tips and advice, but within a month you dropped off and only sent an email once a week, you lied to the good people subscribed to you—*keep your word [5.13]!*

You won't initially develop automations and systems, which means everything you introduce, requires manual effort on your part. Only launch incentives that you intend on keeping and have the sustained mindset to promote.

T: Using a T-chart, list out and categorize the various incentives you are offering or could offer through your personal brand under both free and paid sections.

6.8 | **Transmitting Emotions In Media**

What do the most successful people in the media have in common? Nearly all of them are able to competently transmit their emotions through the content that they appear on or make. They get consumers to feel emotions. I want you to read this next phrase in two different tonalities. The first tone should be emotionless and cold. *"I absolutely love dogs."* Next, actually say it with feeling; you can substitute the word *dog* for anything you care about, *cats, coffee,* or *video games*. Speak with your chest and control your tone of voice to reflect that you actually care. *"I absolutely love dogs."* This is an exercise that not only helps you in reference to public speaking but also as you record audio and video content.

People who conduct interviews don't want to interview somebody who comes across as apathetic or dry. It not only makes for a bad listen, it doesn't do much in the department of confidence. Unless you're a college professor discussing quantum physics, successfully transmitted emotions are more appealing to consume, increase retention and lead to increased engagement.

Transmitting emotions leads others to consume your content and come back for more. If you have already conducted interviews or recorded videos, go back and watch them. How was your overall *stage presence*? When you were sharing a story from your life were you speaking with apathy or conviction?

We have so many forms of media at our disposal, some of which use multiple senses. Video not only appeals to the sense of sight but also your sense of hearing. You must control your tonality and voice, what you're doing with your hands, where you're looking, if you're walking around or standing still, and of the faces and smiles you make.

The greatest public figures transmit emotions via communication methods to trigger a deeper resonance with those on the other end. Actors on the big screen make viewers feel certain emotions and go out of their way to specifically watch movies that they are in. Some are known for being comical and making people laugh, others are more serious, some are almost always in snarky roles, whereas others exclusively play the villain. These archetypes, whether done intentionally or by happenstance, are reflections of what those actors do the best.

As the barriers to entry have decreased and the distribution channels have increased, so has competition. If you were to take two people who say the same exact thing but one of them is a better communicator and strikes emotional chords, which person do you think develops the largest audience, all factors aside?

Human beings are emotional and like to feel connected and comforted by whom they interact. If you are naturally introverted and fall under the more *emotionless* side of the spectrum, I would not encourage you to try too hard to express emotions so that you come across as disingenuous, but I would suggest that you familiarize yourself with letting others in. In the case of the introvert, showing a lack of emotion can actually become a signature as that apathetic nature may be perceived as sarcasm and be used to your benefit; a recent hip-hop interviewer comes to mind.

Imagine a political commentator that doesn't show emotion in the typical outward expressions but approaches political conversations as the smart-aleck. It might just be their greatest selling point.

Transmuting emotions through media helps establish that sought after rapport and exponentially pays off. Do you have something in the way that you communicate that could be your signature? It may also be the case that it develops in time and you don't even realize that you're doing anything out of the ordinary until somebody mentions it to you.

Q: What is your favorite movie or song? Is it your favorite because of the quality of the work or because of the way the work makes you feel?

6.9 | **Good Deeds In Public**

Good deeds are best performed in private and not used as short-sighted ways to boost one's image or visibility. At the time I'm writing the Second Edition, there has been a wave of influencers who have made an entire brand based around feeding the homeless, offering financial donations, and recording other various good deeds. The argument can be made that this is done to spread awareness and to truly contribute something positive for society, but it can also be perceived as an attempt to chase attention.

If you're somebody who cares deeply and wants to perform good deeds, all attention must be directed away from you and onto the cause itself. You can record a video where you give money to a homeless man, but have you once talked about the homelessness issue in your content?

For one of my upcoming projects I will be launching *Mashman Global* to serve as my own philanthropic initiative. I've already partnered up with a wonderful man based out of Ghana and for every dollar of international aid I make, I will also match that to a local cause in the United States. It will all come out of my own pocket and if I'm having a very profitable quarter I can directly help in areas of society that I care about. These areas are: *Education, Entrepreneurship, Health,* and *Quality of Life.*

Mashman Global will never be a source for charity or accept donations. It is exclusively funded by my own ventures. I'm not building my personal brand to be the philanthropic-billionaire type as this idea was actually presented to me by a young gentleman in Ghana, Symuel. Several years ago he asked me to contribute to his Dreamer's Summit in which I recorded a virtual presentation. As we spoke and he mentioned some of the biggest needs that could be found within his local community I could tell that he was coming from a genuine place and wanted to lock arms with a person coming from a place where I have never once missed out on a day of school because I didn't have the proper footwear.

What we end up accomplishing will be an example of good deeds in public but are going to be done in such a way that my intent is evident and it's not some short-sighted attempt to appear as saint-like. Other appropriate ways that you can do good deeds in public would be attending local cleanup events, speaking at colleges relevant to your profession, or making donations in your community after a natural disaster.

Not many people know this, but several years ago a horrible tornado ripped through Little Rock, Arkansas, displacing hundreds of families. I utilized one of the community groups that I was a part of and organized a quick drive for essential goods and items. I took those donations and dropped them off at one of the impromptu Red Cross locations. I made one post on social media about this and left it there. I didn't feel the need to continue basking in something that I would have done without social media. The only reason I mention it here today is to provide you with a real-life example that you may very well find yourself in.

Not everybody needs to see you holding the door for an elderly person or to use the old Boy Scout symbolism, *walking Grandma across the street*. Good deeds should be done out of the kindness of your heart, *nothing more*.

Q: What good deed have you recently done? How did it make you feel? Now imagine if you took to promotion and told others about it. How do you think the emotions would evolve with publicity?

6.10 | **Testing The Waters**

Despite your best efforts at remaining impartial to your actions and progress, a point in time will come where you think your current project or a certain piece of content is damn near perfect. That is, until you talk to a trusted advisor or confidant and they point something out that you completely missed. *Testing the Waters* is about getting advice and opinions from people who want to see you succeed and have little to gain from offering their assistance. These individuals might be farther along than you such as mentors, close business partners, or even friends who have absolutely nothing to do with your business or personal brand. Getting outside perspectives and surveying responses is a great way to catch things that the biased eye tends to overlook.

It's not about getting advice for free or more commonly known as "*trying to pick someone's brain*." These are genuine efforts that come from a place of humility; you are searching for something that will make you better and improve the final outcome. I knew that I could write this book and edit it by myself but I also knew that the most successful books and the ones that go through traditional publishing houses, have editors and in some cases multiple editors. They are outsiders looking in who present new and thoughtful ideas, ways to enhance how sentences and paragraphs are read, and serve to produce a work that is ultimately that much better. This is the reason why I approached my long-time business partner, Eric Chow and asked him to be my editor. I wanted to test the waters and not only benchmark the work that I wrote up until the point I brought him on, but I also wanted to produce something that exceeded the expectations of my readers and that of my First Edition.

The stakes rise as your personal brand scales. If you compare your personal brand to a game of poker, betting $100 might be a lot to the blue-collar man, yet there are big-shot games where hundreds-of-thousands of dollars are on the table. This conversely means that the mistakes you make as your personal brand grows, the larger the ripple effects will be to manage, measure, and understand.

Risk In Relation To Scale

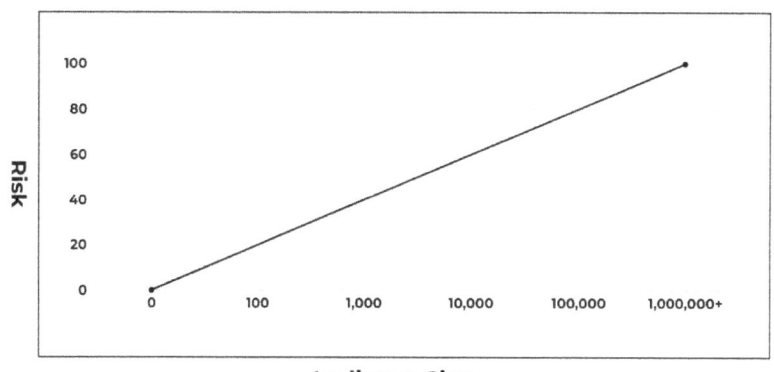

Audience Size

In the line graph above, I use the example of audience size in relation to the percent of risk relative to the degree of public awareness. This serves a purely visual purpose as we would have to collect data such as the quality of demographic, the amount of influence that they collectively have, and so on. There is a clear correlation between the degree of a personal brand's awareness and the degree of risk that is a consequence of any and all mistakes.

For less important matters you can wholly survey your community and ask them which cover art for your upcoming book or podcast they like better, potential names for your new show, and anything else you would like to extend as a formal invitation to be informal contributors of. This can be done either in native polling or posts where you're asking them to comment their thoughts and opinions.

For more important matters, reserve advice to the most trusted individuals in your circle. An added benefit of doing this is they would be more likely to ask you for your own feedback in the future and you'll develop a wonderful synergy that progresses both parties forward.

A: Get into the habit of asking others what better ways you can support them. This is not only a great display of humility that comes from a place of service, but it may also lead to new ideas.

6.11 | **Distribution**

Creating content and producing various forms of media is one of the most time-consuming parts of building an eminent personal brand. *Documentation is easier than creation*, and even then, it requires an extensive amount of conscious action. It's making sure your camera equipment or phone is charged and thinking of relevant things to say when the lens pans your direction; the more established public figure may hire a videographer and foot the travel bills. Documentation is a better use of your time and resources as you're simply making the most out of your day-to-day when by comparison, creating content is more forceful and requires you to stop and film.

The last thing you'd want is to pour all of your effort and emotions into your work just for it to not be seen by anyone. *Enter distribution*. By choosing partners that help with the distribution of your media, you can organically reach broader markets using the platforms your consumers are on and the stores they shop. These partners enhance your authority via association and improve the promotional experience. Remaining exclusive can have its temporary benefits such as marketing nominations, but I would push you to choose *omnipresence* nearly every time.

Imagine walking into your local bookstore and seeing your book on the shelf. Choosing to remain exclusive to one online retailer means that will never happen. Imagine turning on the news and seeing your talk show or opening your podcast player and seeing your podcast. By consequence, you are given the ability to promote it on multiple platforms. Going from an amateur to someone who has a fully developed personal brand requires you to take advantage of these opportunities. Do not discriminate on the size or caliber thereof until several years into your process. The executive may not take every meeting, whereas the early-stage startup founder will. It's the same principle for your personal brand.

Ahead of any launch or release, spend time researching ways you can incorporate mass-distribution. If you find yourself unsure, check forums and consider using AI language models to formulate a plan. As a quick tip, if you use AI in its current form and input sections of this Manifesto, you'll be able to craft an original and effective personal branding strategy.

Artificial Intelligence is worth including as *Artificial Engine Optimization (AEO)* will, in my opinion, become prevalent in the years to come. Are you showing up in these language model's queries? For years the market focused solely on *Search Engine Optimization (SEO)*, tweaking the finest parcel of metadata or changing header elements, but the times have since changed. AI is being built into our phones straight from the factory and we are increasingly reliant on it to answer questions, make calls, and do research without a single shred of doubt in terms of the reliability of its output.

Using Artificial Intelligence to distribute your content is worth factoring if you'd like to get more of your time back. It can be used to automatically respond to messages, benchmark your personal brand, and make and schedule posts; these are but a few of its endless possibilities.

Increase distribution to see more culpable ROIs.

T: Take a look at your current distribution channels and identify narrow areas. Begin to research or hire someone who can help get you into more places.

6.12 | **Selling From Stage**

There's an innate beauty in having one-on-one interactions. The ability to get to know another person and understand them on the deepest level. They establish personal trust and relationships, but are impossible to scale. There's no way for you to be able to have a million different conversations and know a million different people. *This does not infer that a million people cannot know you.*

As your personal brand is established you need to begin thinking about how you can talk to multiple people at once. How can you take your *Elevator Pitch [4.3]* to the masses?

During one of my earliest business trips, I attended a conference hosted by one of social media's largest business figures. I was excited about it and got a great deal on the ticket price, but I wasn't sure what to expect. I knew that after the event I hoped to have received a lot of information from the speakers, but that's about it—*These were renowned celebrity business speakers after all!* In all of my excitement, I brought a pen and binder filled with blank pages. I was taking notes religiously and remained fairly open to new information for the entirety of the event. Much to my despair, I had to read in between the lines of all of the various pitches coming from the podium. It felt like I was witnessing a greedy pastor who spent the entire sermon asking for tithes from the congregation. Years later I came to find out another business mentor I have a stupendous amount of respect for, stopped speaking at many events because of this very kind of experience.

Your intention is not to use public speaking as an opportunity to line your pocketbook. Your intention with selling from stage is to *sell your expertise* and *provide strategic value* to every single person who already paid a premium to be in attendance. If you're on the professional speaking circuit, many event hosts will allow you to pitch your offer at any time during your presentation, however, too much greed will be your downfall and leave people questioning the utility of what they just heard. In my life, the best speeches are those that tell stories and provide tactical advice.

Out of all of the speakers at the event, I only remember several presentations and they ironically came from the people you'd least expect. One was Steve Harvey the renowned comedian and television host, who talked about your gift. I couldn't recite his entire speech by heart but I remember not only how he made me feel but also one of the biggest takeaways; your gift is what comes naturally to you with the least bit of effort. The second speech I remember came from Tai Lopez the *"infamous"* course seller and *"Here in my garage,"* YouTube celebrity. It was amazing seeing him on stage because in real time he was auditing the websites of people in attendance and making proper suggestions that would generate immediate ROI. I was astounded. As for the other speakers...It felt like a pitchfest.

As I am going on to make supplemental income and speak on stages, this subject is at the forefront of my mind as I want to make certain people do not feel like I'm trying to take advantage of them with my position. As a speaker, you automatically are perceived as a person of authority. If you are hosting a conference or Summit and have 10 different speakers, it is unlikely that the person who purchased the ticket will know every single one. What is more likely to happen is they'll purchase the ticket for one or two speakers and the goal is to have those people become so enamored by the others, they're left with their cup running over with knowledge.

The person on stage has all of the attention and leverages the credibility and expertise of every other person who they share the stage with.

For the more intimate events where there are only one or two speakers, the effects of extended association may be limited, but you still have the title of *presenter*. You were either flown out, paid to, or asked to speak whereas everybody else had to go out of their way to purchase their tickets and show up. They trust the event host to provide them with an exceptional experience worthy of their time and money. Do not abuse that gift for it is an honor that few are bestowed.

I am by no means trying to discourage you from taking advantage and making an offer from stage, but if you do, make sure that it aligns with the subject matter in which you just spoke about and is easily accessible. Tie it together with your personal brand and how you want to be positioned. If you are a sales coach delivering a presentation on sales and have a program or exclusive coaching offer, don't make 30 hoops for your prospective students to hop through.

It is about finding and striking a balance between giving and taking. Spend the majority of your time talking about your attendees, and only spend a few minutes at most talking about you. The only exception I would make to this rule is if the stories you're telling are being weaved in such a way that better communicates your message and transmits emotions.

T: Visualize speaking from the stage. What would you speak on and what offer or call to action would you make at the end? Incorporate factors such as the size of the event, demographics, interactions such as Q&As, other panelists, the walk-out music, etc. How would you go about balancing your offer with value?

| 7 |

Personal Skills

Developing the ability to connect with and ultimately influence others

7.1 | **Intrapersonal Relationships**

An *Intrapersonal Relationship* refers to the relationship with oneself. Building your personal brand in a sustainable fashion requires a great degree of dedication, focus, impartiality and self-governance.

To avoid entering into the realm of the *breathing-to-stay-motivated* self-help space, direct your focus towards self-awareness and your internal dialogues. To have as they say, an *"authentic"* personal brand, it must be built off of the back of truthfulness with self and honesty in your actions. People who have poor intrapersonal relationships are often scoped out by the public, but their flaws are often disregarded in exchange for their talents. This might be the alcoholic author, the celebrity who's addicted to drugs or sex, or an obese politician. What they are bringing to the marketplace and offering consumers outweighs their imperfections. Are these flaws what makes their personal brand stand out? Yes, they eventually become a part of their public image, but I wonder if their performance would be that much better if they addressed and improved upon their faults.

Positioning yourself as a public figure requires nearly the same degree of effort if not more than building a business, or getting into the best shape of your life. Running a successful company or having a six-pack may have a positive impact on your personal brand, but these are only extensions and components of it. There is an entire spider web of factors that make up the chemistry of your personal brand similar to that of atoms in the world around us. You are at the center of this massive equation so shouldn't your degree of personal aptitude be one of excellence?

Nobody is going to be there to tell you to attend an event, create content, have conversations, or pitch that reporter. At times you'll be influenced to do certain things, but holistically speaking, self-governance will be the only thing that produces steady progress. It is then up to you to engage in activities that are beneficial to your personal brand and behoove you as the focal point. Such is the fundamental role of self-improvement.

Confidence is only a symptom of action or a lack thereof. A person may be confident in one area of their life such as their physical fitness but be deathly afraid to speak on stage or get in front of a camera. That fitness buff could have fallen in love with health and wellness because they saw their grandparents die young, but their patchy beard or jaw-line makes them hate their appearance. The singer may love to sing because of their favorite musician, but hate dancing out of the fear of injury. Our behaviours are influenced on a daily basis by numerous factors, but we aren't usually aware of how one thing leads to another until well after they happen. Hindsight is *20/20* as they say.

Remaining impartial to your flaws is fundamental to determining the steps that help you move in a favorable direction. Understand your internal dialogues and take note of how you speak to yourself. Having a healthy internal relationship aids in the development of healthy external relationships too, in so much that you do not come across as codependent, desperate, or too reliant on outcomes by the other party.

The desperate salesperson will never sell as much as the person who doesn't communicate their need to make a sale. They could be down to their last dollar and their prospect would never know. Maintaining their composure helps them sell the customer on something they actually need while also solving their personal issues in the process. This is how fruitful partnerships are born. *Out of intent, not out of desperation.*

This concept applies to the dating world and searching for a suitable companion. The man or woman who has a healthy relationship with themself will inherently have standards for the partners they choose. Your intrapersonal relationship affects all areas of your life and you will eventually begin to subconsciously search out methods to strengthen it.

Q: How is your relationship with yourself? What areas can you improve upon to be more efficient at what you do? Are you able to push yourself towards a goal or do you rely on external help? Identify and then formulate a growth plan.

7.2 | **Interpersonal Relationships**

If you were the last person on Earth, you would still technically have a personal brand, but there wouldn't be any power behind it. Nobody to connect with, nobody to entertain or motivate, and nobody to mentor or teach. Other personal brands give purpose and vigor to our own. These *Interpersonal Relationships* are the focus of this subchapter.

Relationships die without mutual effort. Let's look at my relationship with my best friend of more than a decade, Kevin. We went to middle and high school together, I know both of his parents well, and he asked me to be a groomsman at his wedding. He arguably knows me better than anybody else, both my imperfections and where I thrive. Regardless of how tedious life has become, we have always made it a point to stay in contact even if it's through a phone call every couple of months. When we are in person we pick up as if nothing has changed. It is a friendship built off of a foundation of mutual love and expressed brotherhood. Recall the paragraph from *Rapport [4.4]* : "*...upon meeting somebody for the first time, they are on the path to move from being a stranger to an acquaintance, acquaintance to friend, and friend to a best friend.*

A step further and they might even go from being your best friend to what some would consider to be family." We went from being awkward classmates at 11 years old, to viewing each other as family. It took initiative and sustained effort to make it so.

My relationship with my business partner Eric has only improved over the last five years. We have continued to grow together, are always learning about each other, and share common goals. We went from young men doing a podcast to executives building a global business. What relationships from your own life come to mind?

A tree cannot possibly grow without being nurtured by the soil, the sun, and water. To think that you can connect with somebody in a 15-minute networking call and they will automatically become your best friend or an avid supporter is fallacious. As the adage goes, *fortune is in the follow-up* and it applies to relationships the same as it applies to sales. Ask more questions than you are making statements. Express genuine interest in another, learn about their family, their ambitions, their pain points, and in some cases, their childhood and their challenges. Add their birthday to your annual calendar and wish them Happy Birthday and celebrate their anniversaries. Don't wish them a

Happy Holidays for every occasion as it can come across as disingenuous or a backhanded sales attempt of sorts, but in general, people value intentional effort.

We have started to lose the old-world ways of proper face-to-face interactions and sharing authentic experiences. Challenge the norm and adopt the more *"traditional"* or *"unsexy"* aspects from the bygone days.

As time and resources become scarce, there may not be room in your day-to-day life to have as many meetings. When this happens, direct your concentration from one-on-ones to one-to-many. Provide updates on what you are working on and upcoming projects, and be vulnerable enough to talk about stories from your past and their lessons. The internet gives us all the chance to reach billions of people and those that are the most committed and supportive of you, deserve to be informed. *Give your community something to share and advocate for!*

A mentor of mine and fellow personal branding professional Dennis Yu, is known for taking a photo with nearly everybody he comes in contact with. His feed is full of selfies with strangers from various business events, dinners, and his travels. It is his way of giving back and extending his credibility. He has also publicly said it is a way to demonstrate the ease with which content creation can be done. Take more photos with people, have more conversations, ask more questions, and improve your communication skills.

Becoming a master communicator can be as simple as starting conversations with strangers at the grocery store. I make it a point each time I go out to do as many of these actions as I can without turning my trip into a chore:

1. **Give a Compliment:** Find something that you can offer a genuine compliment about that is both respectful and follows societal norms. This could be about their attitude, how the stranger is dressed, the watch they're wearing, or their jewelry or hairstyle. This is the easiest to do and makes the other person feel good about themselves—*how does receiving compliments make you feel?*

2. **Ask a Question:** If a person is looking at a specific product, asking a question can be as down to earth as *"Do you like that brand?"* I'll do this in the coffee aisle and there have

been times when I've been swayed into a purchase because of that random person's perspective. I've also swayed others into purchasing my coffee brand of preference by offering my own insights. It's simple, yet has a tremendous impact on your ability to make conversation out of nothing.

3. **Crack a Joke:** If you feel comfortable enough you can crack a joke about or with a stranger as long as it is well-timed and not ill-mannered. Cracking a joke may come in the form of a shared experience; if you're both standing in line and it's not moving, you could say something along the lines of *"Let me clock in."* This requires more spatial-awareness and taste, but if you can find ways to make a stranger laugh, their guard will instantaneously go down. This is an example of how you can quickly lay down a foundation with those whom you want to know for any length of time.

Your voice is one of your greatest assets in building your personal brand. Audio-only podcasts, one-on-one interactions, recorded video content, and even landing your dream job can all be shaped by your voice. Becoming an effective communicator and understanding your tonalities, the speed in which you're speaking, and the vocabulary you're using are all key aspects that should be audited and polished.

I remember *"pulling my teeth"* and obsessing over my first podcast because of the most minor inconsistencies. I would say *"um"* and use other filler words such as *"like."* To young Isaac they felt like the end of the world but I eventually came to understand that unless these quirks show in every sentence, it's less than likely that others will consciously take notice.

The master communicator is able to describe and share ideas, offer in depth explanations of characteristics, and tell stories in ways most could not. A corporation that is hiring for a client-facing role will choose the better communicator who lacks experience over the experienced introvert who can't talk with major accounts. In my own travels, I have sparked up conversations and met influencers, musicians, planners, other public speakers, real estate brokers and the list goes on. I have gotten comfortable being in situations that others would normally run from.

We could avoid conversations because we don't want to bother someone, we'd simply prefer to stay silent, or we don't have anything to talk about. Giving a stranger a compliment solves the last problem and you'll forever have something to say! Getting good at conversation gives you a leg up and if you can take somebody from being an absolute stranger and in a couple of minutes turn them into an acquaintance, the opportunities are endless.

Q: Which of the aforementioned strategies do you need the most practice with?

7.3 | **Networking and Introductions**

Introversion doesn't have a place when it comes to building your personal brand. One of my earliest business endeavors was in the industry of Network Marketing. After joining three companies, on four separate occasions, I eventually left the industry to build something more in my control without the stipulations and labels. From my short time in the field, I took away some valuable lessons in how to become a master at networking. There are four questions that you should ask in order to develop an increased awareness of the other person. This additional information can be used in relation to building rapport, giving gifts, and sales. These questions take the acronym of **FORM**:

- **Family:** The purpose of asking about family is not to learn all of their relatives' names or their full life story. Inquiring about family, which tends to be one of the most important aspects to a person, gives you a lot of information on their past experiences, their environments, and quite possibly their motivations. Were their parents also practicing professionals in their current industry? Do they have any children and are they married? This context enables you to make more informed decisions on their boundaries and when they might be unavailable to take a call, be asked for advice, and what they'd be interested in.

- **Occupation:** What is their current profession and why did they get started in the field? You can use this time to ask about their work experiences and all of the other attempts and career choices they have made. Understanding their occupation is a quintessential part of knowing how you can best support and serve them. Recall the subchapter on *Building Your Contact List [6.4]*. Although you might not immediately need their products or services, you could still keep them in your referral network.

- **Recreation:** It's all too common to spend time talking about work and no time talking about fun. Asking what hobbies and passions they engage in on their downtime offers a fresh change of pace and is an opportunity to find ground for rapport. Do they like to travel? If they're in great shape you can probably assume that they spend a lot of time in the gym. Do they enjoy bicycling, hiking, or going out to trivia? Whatever it is, you will conceivably find that you share some interests. Having this piece of information makes giving custom-tailored gifts personable and *"From the heart."*

- **Motivation:** Uncovering a person's motivations on first approach may appear to be somewhat intrusive, but it isn't in practice. If you already know about their *family, occupation,* and *recreational activities* you would have uncovered aspects of what is pushing them forward. Tapping into their emotions is the closest thing to seeing their true self. During my client consultations, I'll ask them to share their biggest goals that they would feel uncomfortable sharing with their friends and family out of the fear of criticisms or objections. I cut straight to the point and ask the difficult questions. Once they're out of the way, everything that follows pales in comparison.

In the course of networking, it is not your place to criticize, judge, or object to another. Networking is purely the gathering of information, finding pieces of connection, and laying the foundation for a forthcoming relationship. It is a time of fellowship, not a time to be adversarial in the slightest sense.

As you ask questions, curiosity develops in the other person's mind. They will begin asking questions of their own which is indicative that your conversation is flowing well. Take the time to get their contact information before you walk off and if it's somebody that you have serious interest in developing a relationship with, proceed to message them within minutes of walking away, simply thanking them for their time.

Implementing the *Power of 3* [6.5] might only increase your personal brand's reach by 1,095 people in the first year, but what happens in year two is astounding. You will have developed strong enough relationships that they will begin to share your content, tell their friends and associates, and become your greatest advocates. They are in the market of *second-degree connections* which are simply people that you are not personally connected with, but have a relationship with somebody who is. *It is easier (and better) to be introduced than it is to try and introduce yourself without edification—formal praises.* Introductions are how you figuratively *skip the line* and go straight into the realm of another.

If you would like to get in contact with a particular person, an industry leader perhaps, you might have somebody in your network who is their associate or friend. There is nothing wrong with asking them to make an introduction, as long as you have built a relationship with the person you're asking the favor of. Upon doing so, communicate your intent. Why are you asking for the introduction? Give them a reason to approach the professional and never ask for an introduction for introduction's sake. *Have a purpose behind it!* If it's too early and there isn't an immediate need, consider waiting until you're in a more suitable place. The last thing you want people to do is waste your time, so why would you waste another's?

Introductions are a form of edification and endorsement so expect to reciprocate the favor should you be asked. You have an obligation to yourself and a duty to the person making the introduction to hold yourself to a proper standard and not betray their good faith. If you do fall short, your best hope is to get ahead of it, hold yourself accountable, and fix your mistakes. Your actions are affecting not only how you are perceived by the third-party, but the person who introduced you as well. It is up to you to live up to your promises, adhere to your word, and be a person worthy of edification.

A: As you begin networking and sharpening your communication skills, direct your conversations to learn about their family, occupation, recreation, and motivations. Put the acronym *FORM* front and center in your mind.

7.4 | **Being Magnetic**

Accomplishments automatically attract people to you and sometimes for the wrong reasons. A person might believe that they can boost their credibility, have exclusive experiences, progress their personal agendas, or reap financial benefits, etc; just by association. It isn't your place to cast judgment but to exercise acceptance on the nature of this fact.

Despite what much of the public believes, being a person of interest does not automatically translate to being financially successful. This is a fallacy in which society has crafted—See *Dangers of Influence [3.8]*. Not all celebrities are rich, not all comics write their own jokes, and not all actors perform their own stunts. If you'd like to attract the right people, get the most out of your efforts, and have strong relationships, it's required that you cultivate *Personal Magnetism*.

Personal magnetism is more symbolic than anything as for the sake of humor it's not like you have a North and South Pole, but there is truth in considering the aura certain individuals create. Presidents like Barack Obama and Donald J. Trump have been said to make anybody who comes in contact with them feel as if they are the most important person in the world. It's a way of directing all of the attention and energy to another. Some of this *feeling* is absolutely influenced by their *power*, both political and professional, but magnetism itself is generated through many of the strategies that we've covered. From asking questions and showing interest, to becoming a master communicator and edifying those that deserve to be edified.

Personal magnetism is generated by the fabric of your being which casts a sense of importance, prowess, and public relevance. When you go to a large-scale event, you'll notice when the speaker walks in everybody in the audience falls silent and directs their attention towards them. It is not only out of respect, but also a platonic attraction. That very speaker who has yet to say one word, commands the attention of the room. *This is personal magnetism at work.*

I observed this phenomenon during my first-ever business trip. The Vice President of the company I was a distributor for, walked into the room, wearing bright red pants, a beautiful blazer, and sparkling sneakers. On his wrist was a bedazzled Rolex watch and his hair was freshly cut and combed to the side. I remember more about how he made me feel than his speech itself. The way you dress, the way you sit, the way you stand, the way you speak, the tattoos you do or do not have, and virtually everything else that you can think of contributes to your personal brand and how you are shaping your public image; all of which are aspects of your personal brand that your competitors are not remotely considering.

On that same business trip, I was one of the only distributors who came dressed in a full suit. Where others were more interested in the Vice President's Rolex I was more interested in the knowledge he was teaching. Their shortsightedness allowed me to spark a conversation that easily stood out. I told him my story of buying a one-way bus ticket from Jacksonville, FL to New York City, the 70 hours of travel time, sleeping on the floor, and so on. He was impressed and invited not only myself, but my entire team to an exclusive leaders' dinner. I exercised personal magnetism which resulted in a rare opportunity that I cherish to this day. Bold but earnest confidence helps obtain all of the outcomes you desire.

A: Work on increasing your personal magnetism. Give thought to changing hairstyles, refreshing your wardrobe, and building the confidence to be the center of attention.

7.5 | **Reading Intentions**

Skepticism serves an instinctual purpose. It's in our nature to question things that we aren't familiar with or understand. When we meet a stranger for the first time, we don't know if the person we are speaking to has an agenda, is a serial killer, is trustworthy, or if they're honestly talking to us for what we would deem to be a good reason. It's impossible to know everything going on in that individual's mind but we have to do our best to read their intent. We should never change our character of being to try and adapt to another's expectations. *This isn't a game of make-believe or play pretend.*

There is no need to be so skeptical that you become a hermit living on a mountainside or are completely detached from civilization, but there is verity to becoming better at reading intentions. This is especially true when you get to a higher place in life, command more influence, have more followers, and are reflected by the numbers in your bank account. Personal magnetism attracts all sorts of people.

When somebody approaches you with a business deal that at first glance appears to be "*Too good to be true,*" are you automatically going to take their word at its face value or will you take the time to do due diligence and come to conclusions of your own? When a young professional in your field, whether that be acting, blue-collar services, litigating, etc, approaches you and offers to take you out to dinner you can safely assume that they want to pick your brain. Is this something you want to do and do you have the time to expend?

One of my clients reached out to me the other day and asked to do just that. Now we're in different states so he didn't offer to buy me dinner, but he asked if I would spend some time brainstorming with him. I had to politely decline and set a boundary. There were multiple reasons that I factored into my decision and it wasn't that I was ignoring him, I was occupied. I was already spending an immense amount of time helping his wife publish her book and I couldn't see myself being able to offer that kind of support at that current moment. I let him know these things but left him with a word of encouragement and told him that he needed to spend time discovering and failing himself. I wanted to see more effort on his end to become self-sufficient and exercise intrapersonal skills. When he does this, maybe my response will be different in the future.

He was not malicious and if anything, his intent was in all of the proper places, but I also knew that I had the ability and right to object. If you choose to object to opportunities, do so with class and respect. If you are certain that somebody has the ill-conceived intent to harm or take advantage of you, you do not owe an explanation; you do not have to respond, but if you choose to do so, do not attack them. *It isn't worth the time or energy.*

T: With the sole purpose of identifying intentions, look through the last 10 conversations you've had with other people. Were they trying to genuinely spend time with you? Maybe they wanted to get more for less or had the intention of hiring you. Were their compliments genuine or meant to lower your guard? Do not approach this as a skeptic or read too deeply into these conversations, this is merely meant to increase your awareness as future interactions occur.

7.6 | **Negotiating On Your Behalf**

Being approached with offers are common occurrences within an established and growing personal brand. This could include being asked to speak at an event, contributing to a documentary, endorsing a product, partnering up for an upcoming project, a sponsorship deal, and other examples that are relevant to your industry. Hence learning to *Negotiate On Your Behalf* is a fundamental skill you must learn.

Negotiating on your behalf is also determining your pricing in relation to your deliverables. Several months ago I was approached by somebody who was looking to network. I obliged and we hopped on a phone call where we spoke for a little over 10 minutes. As it turns out he was interested in growing his personal brand and I had him do some research into what I had accomplished. By now, many of my successes are self-evident and I wasn't trying to convince him of anything nor was I even trying to sell him. He proceeded to claim that where he was in his life in relation to his personal brand was better than my own. As he was saying these things, I privately performed an audit. Not only were his social media pages disorganized and unkept, his handles were different, there was no consistent branding or marketing, and the press features he claimed to legitimately have obtained appeared to be bought.

It was with further research that I saw he had recently published a book. Self-publishing any text is easy to do as the barrier to entry is low and as long as you have something to say or use artificial intelligence, you can become a published author in less than a week. This is quite different from previous eras where you would've had to go through a traditional publisher. If I recall correctly, he published his paperback and was charging over $40 for a book that was under 100 pages. The amount of ego this gentleman possessed astounded me. Needless to say, he removed me from social media and two weeks later a virtual assistant reached out through his profile to ask me to support something he had going on. *Ludicrous.*

His paperback may have contained wonderful text and value, but he didn't know how to negotiate on his behalf without coming across as a complete jerk—he made a fool of himself. Learning this skill is not only about taking into account where you are in your journey, but is also about recognizing the value that you can provide concerning the offer and the possibilities standing in front of you. In a later subchapter, *Building A Team [8.5]*, I discuss this in greater detail.

A substantial issue with people who are working to build their personal brand and are particularly driven by money and vanity, is that they lose sight of the bigger picture. *They think that they are bigger than they actually are.* If you're just starting out, you shouldn't be asking a brand for $100,000 to make a sponsored post or sell a product.

Household names are able to demand such a large compensation but have supporting evidence to back up their requests. *You can still get paid quite well if your focus is put on the deliverables you're providing to the other party.* There are many ways to structure a deal. Instead of asking for a lump sum upfront, you could become an affiliate partner and get paid a percentage every time a person uses your code or says that you referred them to the company or product. You could get paid on a month-to-month basis on retainer and the more established public figure who has a degree of business success, might even ask for equity.

Approach offers that come to your desk without greed. See them through to the end and deliver what you promised to the best of your abilities. I would suggest that you book a consultation with a lawyer to ensure that any endorsements or deals that you are being compensated for are done within the legal boundaries of the law.

Never sell out your personal brand for something you don't even use. Advertising laws are ever-changing and relative, and as the internet matures more regulations and rules will be implemented. The last thing you want is to be caught up in a court case because you deceivingly promoted something in exchange for compensation. Honesty helps you avoid most pitfalls.

You'll eventually find yourself negotiating time itself such as the expectations for attending an event and how much time you can devote for interviews. Be reasonable with your approach and if you feel like you're not being fairly compensated or worked with, it is your prerogative to withdraw given no contracts are signed. You might ask for more than the initial offering and when doing so have your reasons straight and see if your requests can be accommodated.

Asking for what you feel like you deserve is much better than providing a less-than-exceptional experience because you weren't fairly compensated in your mind.

A: The next time you are at a restaurant or purchasing something, ask for an employee discount or a better rate. Get comfortable asking for preferential outcomes even if you don't expect it to work.

| i |

Identity Positioning: A Macroscopic View on Personal Branding

In September of 2024, I wrote and published this academic paper Identity Positioning: A Macroscopic View on Personal Branding as almost an intermissionary piece from the release of the First and Second Editions of my Manifesto. For your convenience, I have included an unaltered copy below. I chose to put it before the chapter "Sustainability" as it is a good summation of what we've discussed thus far. Identity Positioning will become a central personal branding standard in the coming years.

With the creation and adoption of technology over the last two decades such as social media, personal video at scale, and artificial intelligence, the consumer market has evolved drastically. Whereas the barrier of entry to be a celebrity was extremely high for the entirety of the 20th century, now through social media and content creation, anybody can go from a nobody to an influential somebody. From having zero followers to audiences of millions in a relatively short amount of time. This can be dehumanizing, making these interactions feel superficial.

These shifts in the market have led to the mass adoption of endorsement marketing where everybody, including their grandparents, wants to be an influencer. It's no longer a movie star advertising Old Spice or Marilyn Monroe wearing Chanel perfume. There is this desire, whether driven by vanity, money, or mission, to become famous and at the very least have successful personal brands. In parallel, more ranking executives are choosing to become front-facing and serve as public representatives for their corporations. It conversely humanizes what were once bland corporations run by men in black suits. Interestingly, the CEOs or founders often have larger audiences than the businesses themselves.

Personality sells.

Upon observing the rapid changes in our consumer behavior, I developed what I believe is the next evolution of personal branding. I call my approach **Identity Positioning**, and it is the one thing many people today lack. It merges the personal identity of the individual with their professional career in such a way that crafts public authority, demonstrates competence, develops a loyal following, and is effective regardless of how the world landscape changes. This is a philosophy in so much as it is a strategy and will be the standout approach for years to come.

Whether you are finding yourself lost in this new generation of advancement, or are looking to attain a certain outcome by being a part of the leaders, not the consumers, I hope my study will lead you to be more effective in your own personal brand's progression and offer new perspectives on the subject.

What Is Personal Branding?

The first widely known use of the term *"personal brand"* can be found in Tom Peters' article for *FastCompany*, *"The Brand Called You."* For being written in 1997, Tom was way ahead of the curve. Most who use the phrase "personal brand" don't know that it was only coined within the last three decades. This particular piece is worth reading and is foundational for much of the work that is done in the space today. Although Peters put a lot of emphasis on professional characteristics in more of a corporate-America setting, I believe it served its purpose when it was written and the impact it has had is undeniable. I'd like to expand on Mr. Peters' work and usher in the next era of personal branding, more appropriate for the ever-evolving time we live in.

In my professional life, I've had the pleasure of consulting clients from numerous industries and verticals such as authors, business owners, coaches, consultants, creators, entertainers, models, podcasters, public speakers, and more. I am proud to say that my approach has always been identifying my clients' personal traits and interests while seamlessly combining them with their professional careers and outlook. Over the last decade, I have sought depth in my work—some sort of secret sauce that helps me feel like we are digging deeper than the surface and focusing on the broader approach of an individual's image.

Where Personal Brand Professionals Go Wrong

I find most of my competitors in the space, who also provide personal brand coaching or consulting in some official capacity, usually lack substance in terms of their vision. They focus on micro-strategies, addressing one or two concerns without taking into account a broader approach to their client's needs and ambitions. They make suggestions like *"Let's grow your social media page"* but won't discuss how they're being perceived. Work to have them show up on Google, yet avoid getting their clients a personal website. This is why, at large, I only consume a little content, if at all, from others in my space. Additionally, many times my *"colleagues"* implement short-term strategies themselves, paying for awards and press, rather than becoming press-worthy. You aren't in the business of convincing, but rather in demonstrating.

There's a common phrase in sales that states *'people do business with whom they know, like, and trust.'* If this is the case, why is so much emphasis put on professional accolades and marketing messages, yet the most crucial aspects are nowhere to be found? People write sales scripts such as *"I help coaches make X amount of revenue in Y time frame"* and *"Working with so-and-so clients to get so-and-so results"* and expect it to convert. They rarely showcase their *human* side out of fear that it would affect their broader *'image'* oftentimes limiting their phrasing and creation strictly to their professional career like an uptight lawyer.

While it is true that showing too much of your personal life without showcasing your professional experiences may affect the psychological distance between you and the other person, what if there was a better way? A balance to strike? This is why, after observing these trends, I created a revolutionary approach which combines both philosophical and strategic elements to allow anyone to position themselves as a public figure worth following, liking, and trusting—somebody who can be in demand and serve as an authority while also being down to earth.

When I made the decision to consciously build my personal brand everything changed. I don't come from a well-known family, I didn't have mentors around me who could guide me on this new path, and I lacked the tools that I needed to grow. I had to build myself up as much as I had to build my personal brand. I lacked public significance but followed every step that I laid out for you in this thought piece. I prefer this macroscopic view because it offers security and room for expansion. It doesn't matter if one marketing platform disappears, your account gets removed, or other divine interventions change the tools at your disposal. Having a personal brand that is well-rounded and reflects YOU will encompass all the other avenues as extensions.

How I Have Used Identity Positioning For My Personal Brand

In the early days of my career, I went from business to business, searching for my vehicle. My stress was exacerbated by not fully understanding *who I was*. Through my study, I knew obscurity was the enemy of success, ultimately leading me to build out my personal brand online in the least, as this ambitious young entrepreneur. In every new endeavor I got myself involved in, I had to my surprise, people supporting me. Why was that? It wasn't because I was some sort of authority. I didn't have the experience to become one. It was because they connected with me, Isaac Mashman. They saw my vision and that I was working on finding something greater for myself. They latched onto this and lived vicariously through me.

By the time I figured out what my vehicle was, I had a series of thousands of people who helped me get started, launch, and then build. It didn't matter if I was in a network marketing company, the music industry, podcast management, or a different avenue—they wanted to see me win. I built a connection with strangers on the internet that I eventually transmuted into a faithful following. I use the term faithful not in a religious sense, but in that it denotes avid support. If you ask your followers to do something, they happily oblige. Your CTAs *(Calls-to-Action)* convert because it's a friend who is asking, not a stranger.

Practical Application In Marketing Messages

Imagine the word *"personal brand"* is split into two so it appears as **PERSONAL || BRAND**. On the left side, you have the word *"personal."* This consists of the characteristics, interests, hobbies, passions, traits, life experiences, and other aspects of an individual. It's what makes them that unique friend to have—the same reason some students get labeled the class clown or the most likely to succeed. On the right, you have *"brand."* This side is reserved for accomplishments, certifications, professional careers, years of service, testimonials, and things that generate revenue or attention in an industry-specific way. An immense number of people focus on the right side—the brand—and not so much on the person themselves.

Let us take the marketing message *"I help X people get Y results."* Starting with the words *"I help"* denote service and intimacy, but what if you added a personal hook to that marketing message? *"Avid outdoorsman and loving father. I help X people get Y results."* This small amount of context gives a prospective follower or buyer information that establishes rapport.

Rapport is trust, and in the digital space, it's not like you are literally shaking another person's hand and they're able to look you in your eyes and intuitively read you. However, you do have the ability to leave a first impression. The fact that the person is a fan of the outdoors and is a father gives two rapport pieces that similar professionals wouldn't have publicly displayed. This method helps visualize the *identity* of the person much more effectively, *positioning* them as someone trustworthy and personable. It applies to the nerdy business owner to the quirkily dressed musician.

To properly understand **Identity Positioning**, and create a successful personal brand, there are four pillars that we need to go through to properly set a foundation.

Education: *Understanding What Your Personal Brand Is*

Without understanding what your personal brand is, your perspective will be shortsighted. Your personal brand is YOU! Every single thing about you—from the place you were born, your career, your political affiliation, your faith, etc. It is not something that is only created because of technology and the internet. I could go completely off the grid electronically speaking tomorrow, and still go to my local Chamber of Commerce and connect with other business leaders. I could still provide services despite lacking an online presence. Combining both offline and online tactics is the hidden weapon that will create the greatest results in this new techno-social period. Understanding this pillar gives you a broad perspective that others lack and a deeper resonance in your *identity*.

Mindset: *The Mindset of the Public Figure*

We have to think BIG. I need your comfort zone to be challenged and here's why. There are nearly 4 billion people today who are on the internet, if not more. Even if a fraction of those people are on the creating end of the spectrum, that is an immense amount of competition you are fighting to get attention with. I believe with the increasing accessibility of technology in hubs such as India and Africa, we will soon see a rise in more geographically centered influencers.

You should be positioned as an authority and as a public figure. You have to be the person that other people know and respect. There's no other way in today's age to combat this without losing out on opportunities. There will come a point where more people know about you, and you don't even know they exist.

You could be approached in public by somebody who has been following you for years and knows information about you, yet you might not know the first shred of details about them. A remarkable thought, isn't it? This phenomenon is best seen in the celebrity realm. You likely know a lot of facts about your favorite movie star, but they wouldn't know your first name. Managing your thinking in this pillar will help you set realistic expectations and why *positioning* is so important.

Branding: *Who You Are and How You Position Yourself*

Knowing now that you have to be a public figure, how do you position yourself as such? This is where strategies that contribute to your credibility come into play.

Some of these are as follows:
- Receiving features and quotes in the press
- Podcast interviews
- Traditional forms of media communication such as radio and television appearances
- Creating content on your industry and subject matter
- Authorship
- Public speaking
- Writing articles and columns
- Associating with other leading professionals.

You are looking for ways to make yourself stand out and for third-party edification.

Edification is where another person talks highly about you, validating your claims. You can say that you are the greatest expert, but that comes across with bias. The expert is identified through other people vouching for them and is usually perceived better in terms of public opinion. Outside of being you, what do you want to be known for? A high-ticket consultant, an industry-leading public speaker, a loving advocate? Having an outcome in mind enables you to cut through the noise more easily and reverse engineer steps to get there, assisting in how you *position* yourself. Now it's about getting more awareness, hence, the fourth pillar of **Identity Positioning**, Marketing.

Marketing: *How You Get More People To Know About You*

Marketing is arguably the easiest step of this process because every interaction that gets somebody to know about you is an example—from the handshake with a barista to advertisement campaigns to the strategies that I talked about earlier that contribute to your positioning.

It can be as simple as *The Power of 3 [6.5]*. Connecting with 3 new people every day for a year will grow your network by 1,095 people. Your ultimate goal with marketing yourself and your personal brand is to get more people to hear your name, and be introduced to what you stand for.

From there, the content and tasks that you are doing enable that new fan or follower to learn information about what *you* have going on. Being educated in potential marketing channels gives you a competitive advantage in reaching more people who would latch on to your *identity*.

Examples of marketing strategies are:
1. The Power of 3
2. Direct marketing
3. Social media
4. Email marketing
5. Podcasting, both host and interviewee
6. Press features and quotes
7. Television and radio appearances
8. Attending events
9. Paid advertising

The Law of Familiarity

There is what I call the Law of Familiarity. This Law refers to strangers becoming acquaintances and eventually becoming avid supporters. Think back to your first day of school. It always felt awkward at first, but by the end of the year, you had your friends, you knew everybody and they knew you. You knew your classes and teachers and were familiar. Your personal brand gets people familiar with *the business of you*. Edification is effective because the person providing the edification is familiar to their audience. You are going into the conversation with a stranger and by introduction are leaving a vetted figure.

The Overarching Reasons Why You Want To Build Your Personal Brand

Like a holding company is an umbrella for all of the businesses underneath it, there are three overarching reasons why somebody would build out their personal brand.

Vanity

Simply put, people like attention. They like being recognized and want to be known for vanity or greed. This isn't a discussion on the moral ramifications of personal branding, but oftentimes entertainers especially like the idea of being famous. It makes you feel good!

Money

Constructing your personal brand can be a fantastic vehicle for generating revenue. You can utilize your personal brand to drive awareness towards a business, receive compensation through sponsorships or affiliates, and get paid to speak on stage. Monetizing your personal brand is a fantastic testament to success and accomplishment. The consultant starting out might only be able to charge $100 per consultation, but as their reputation grows and their personal brand scales, they can eventually charge as much as, or even more than, $10,000 for an hour's worth of their time. They have a track record of results.

Mission

Some may be driven by a sense of mission and purpose. They understand that the larger they become, so does their ability to drive awareness to a cause they care about. This can be seen in the non-profit space with billionaire philanthropists. They are associating themselves with causes that they believe in and can put out calls to action for their audiences to do the same.

In your personal brand journey, you may be driven by one of or a combination of these three overarching reasons. It's important to note that they may be less or more influential than the others. Most of the time, people are held back because, number one, they do not know the reasons they are building their personal brand, or number two, they do not know where to get started.

Identity Positioning offers flexibility. It doesn't matter if your driving reasons change, the person doesn't. Of course, there's a buffer for your evolution, but it's unlikely people will stop supporting you unless some major personality fluctuations take place.

How You Can Leverage Identity Positioning For Your Personal Brand

In leveraging **Identity Positioning**, and combining those personal and professional attributes, you are openly showcasing who you are and why they may be interested in aligning their lives with your own. Building your personal brand is the equivalent of building a business. What expectations for consumers are you setting? When you purchase a particular product or service from a business, you are expecting a certain outcome. You have been influenced over the years by so many marketing messages and decisions, from an entity's branding to the fact that Coca-Cola was your grandmother's favorite drink, ultimately leading you to make a purchasing decision. We are subconsciously influenced from the time we were children and as memories develop so do our biases.

What expectations are you setting for your personal brand? Your personal brand is not something that is built, optimized, or scaled overnight, rather is a continual process. I would argue you have had your personal brand from the moment you came out of your mother's womb. Your parents named you, determined where you were born, your associations and affiliations, and your beliefs. They nurtured into you all of those various aspects that make you who you are today, and your environment, your nature. That failed business you had, the degree you worked so hard for, your romantic pursuits, and so on.

Answer the following questions:

1. What are you looking to gain from consciously establishing your personal brand? Is it vanity *(seeking recognition)*, money, or mission *(promoting causes)*? Once you understand what is driving you, go

through the four pillars and familiarize yourself with what they stand for. Seeing positive outcomes will only motivate you to take it more seriously.

2. Identify what you want to be known for. See the branding pillar for reference. Are you showing your personal side or limiting yourself to pure professionalism? It may take some time to strike a balance.

3. What are some easy and free marketing vehicles you can use to get more people to know about you? Test out strategies over the next several months and adjust them accordingly.

4. Reverse engineer other leaders who have similar results to what you want. This is one of the best ways to find the best path forward.

Skyline Strategy

Implement the *"Skyline Strategy"* – For every 2 steps that grow the *brand* side, take 1 that grows your *personal*. All great cities have beautiful skylines. What does yours look like? In terms of videos that I record, I try to adhere to this 2:1 ratio to the best of my ability. I may record two videos about my consultancy or public relations, followed by one story from my past or of me doing things in my day-to-day life like bicycling or hiking. I add context to the man. City skylines are constructed over time. Sometimes skyscrapers are added, other times they're demolished. Don't be afraid to switch up your marketing or pivot as you see fit. Sit down with pen and paper and come up with ideas for content. Draw a T chart and categorize where that idea falls under. Personal or Profession? All consumed media does 4 things: *Educates, Entertains, Inspires/Motivates, and Connects.*

Examples of *personal* content are:
- Vlogs and "Day in the Life" videos
- Personal anecdotes
- Your day-to-day experiences like dinner, working out, your lifestyle
- Serious hobbies

Examples of *brand* content are:

- DIY tutorials
- Professional anecdotes
- Education oriented
- Client stories
- Career challenges

By diversifying your content, you are bridging the gap between you as the creator and the consumer. You must speak with enthusiasm and exhibit your personality. No one wants to follow a bore.

Using This Gift

Your personal brand is a gift. It is something that you should cherish and respect. As your influence grows in magnitude, the more leverage you have to get opportunities to come to you rather than search for those opportunities yourself. You want to become sought after and set forth public commitments that you can use for personal gain. Have a foundation set in moral beliefs and follow the ethics of modern civilization to build for the long term.

Growing your personal brand is a lifetime endeavor. Be on the lookout for *cracks in your foundation*. Risks that could grow into something bigger. Address concerns as they come, associate with the right people, and what you wouldn't talk about with associates, friends, and family, don't talk about publicly. The smallest of efforts stack up.

If you apply the principles of **Identity Positioning** you will assuredly stand out in this hypercompetitive environment and develop your own personal brand in such a way that leaves lasting impressions of increase, attracts opportunities, and helps you achieve your aspirations.

As your results compound, reach out and let me know how **Identity Positioning** has helped you!

Do not abuse this gift, as it takes hundreds of years for the mightiest oak tree to be nurtured and grown, but only minutes for it to get cut down. Such is the qualm of reputation.

So, *who are you?*

| 8 |

Sustainability

Information and strategies to help you sustain your personal brand throughout your life

8.1 | Integrity, Etiquette, and Taking Credit

Integrity is about doing the right thing even when nobody's watching. Nobody will see all the offers that get presented to you, the opportunities that you turn down, or the backdoor deals that you could have taken. An example in concordance to the time this book is being published is that of cryptocurrency coins. Celebrities and influencers are being approached by coin developers and are being asked to promote something that has no intrinsic value; it's purely based on arbitrage for profit. These scammers have the goal of making a lot of money in a very short time. They tell the celebrity or influencer that they'll get paid a certain amount upfront and by promoting these coins, all they have to do is say that their account was hacked or claim ignorance. This only happens after both parties walk away rich with ponzi profit. *What a betrayal of trust.*

A successful personal brand has the ability to move mountains with the snap of their fingers and the words coming from their mouth, but this gift comes with a cost. You must be more thoughtful in every decision you make. I hope that you do not use this book as a manual for abuse. Machiavelli's work has been taken out of context by many, yet if you approach it with an open, less critical mind, you realize Niccolo was never once advocating for amoral behaviors. He provided examples of princes during his era that rose to power and their unethical practices, but he discouraged the reader from doing so themselves. My work is quite similar in that regard.

Your personal brand opens up a vast world of leverage and manipulation which can easily be abused by less-than-good characters. A government builds out its military not with the intent of ever having to use it, but rather as a preventative measure and show of force should other countries seek to attack or take advantage. It's a deterrent more than it is a weapon. Just because you can do something doesn't always mean you should, especially if it sacrifices your integrity and leads to a negative outcome for the people who are supporting you. As we are covering *Integrity*, I'd like to extend our conversation to include how to take credit.

The team of researchers who make discoveries with their experiments are almost always credited as being a part of the project—why shouldn't you? Taking credit is less about boasting over your work and is more about publicly displaying your competency and efforts. Asking for accreditation is not a show of ego, but of respect for yourself and towards those you're working alongside with, or for. The designer who crafts best-selling cover art is mentioned under the copyright page and in some cases on the cover itself. Alexander Stephens, the mastermind behind the fingerprint and design of my Manifesto is mentioned under my photo on the physical copy. The person in the studio who contributed even one word to a song is listed as a writer within its metadata. The voice narrator of a documentary is credited on IMDb.

Credits contribute to your body of work, making it easier to pursue future projects. True professionals want to see your abilities on display and receive notes of confidence with your promises. Receiving proper credits will likewise, increase the percentage chance of being discovered. Our world relies a great deal on algorithms and chance. The owner must publicly say that they're the founder of their business and if you run a search on any notable entity, you'll find an abundance of information on their executive teams. *Taking credit is putting that with which you've labored so hard for, to work for you.*

Before embarking on a new undertaking, there is nothing wrong in asking about being able to publicly use your part in the project for future marketing materials and in properly defining your association therein. It makes you feel uncomfortable the first several times, but eventually becomes a common part of your checklist. If the referenced endeavor does not allow you to publicly lay claim, it is up to you to decide if you're willing to trade your talent and time for a payday. I have found in most situations, asking and having these discussions boosts their feelings towards you and communicates a sense of ambition, equaled with appreciation. Giving credit to all parties involved also increases the visibility of marketing channels.

In terms of your past works that you weren't credited for or never discussed the intricacies of, reach back out to the decision-makers and get clarity. A contract that outlines given permissions is worth considering, especially for larger enterprises. After you've received the green light, begin to promote them! This can be done in a variety of ways that don't convey narcissism such as:

- **"Did you know that I...."** — Asking this interactive question engages your community while bringing recognition to the venture. This is the least effective of the four included methods.

- **"When I was working on XYZ, I had such and such funny experience."** — This format brings awareness to the project, demonstrates aspects of your personality, and offers insights into what are typically private environments. Think about the movie star who tells a story from the set.

- **"A lesson I learned from doing XYZ"** — By sharing a piece of wisdom, you display growth and tell your audience you participated in a project.

- **"I'm proud to announce that..."** — You use your credit as a tool for promotion, simultaneously driving traffic and boosting your authority. Approaching an announcement with respect should be reserved for notable achievements that will *'turn heads.'*

Taking credit is about acknowledging your work and talents, and isn't a window to boast. **Never take credit for something you don't deserve.** *Intellectual Property Theft* and *Infringement* falls under the same category as defamation. Your claims of ownership or your part in, must be backed by evidence. How you handle your accomplishments is almost as important as getting the accomplishment itself. If you make it all about you and come across as too self-praising, it leaves a bad taste in the mouths of others. Instead of being the accomplished man or woman that has class and respect for their hard work, they'll be perceived as full of themselves. It is impossible to please everybody, that much is known, but it doesn't mean you should make more enemies or do harm to your reputation.

If your long-term goal has been to be featured in or quoted by a major media outlet and you made it happen this year, you're not going to go around to everybody saying *"Look at me I got featured in X!"* Instead, tastefully promote your feature, add words of encouragement to your copy, discuss how you were able to land such a feature in the first place, highlighting any major takeaways. You don't go to a fine dining restaurant wearing basketball shorts and you don't curse around elderly people. These are more than formalities, they're proper ways of behavior that represent appreciation and respect for the subjects at hand.

The right people will appreciate your accomplishments given you don't shove it in their face. This is proper etiquette and sets an example. Forcefully promoting your accomplishments gives off the appearance that you didn't think that you deserved them and that you're not good enough. *Don't be surprised—It's what you wanted all along, isn't it?*

Q: Who comes to mind when you think about people who sacrificed their integrity in exchange for an opportunity or payday?

8.2 | **When You Lack Expertise Or Skills**

Every person who reads this will be at a different point in life. You might be in high school, fresh out of college, or a retired 60-year-old professional who wants to mentor the masses and share your decades' worth of experience and expertise. I would like to speak to the person who is just starting and in their mind might be *"a nobody."* I didn't begin knowing anything about business, reputation management, personal branding, or taxes. I was guided by mentors, some in-person and some virtual. I encountered challenging experiences and had hard lessons to learn. I started building my brand as an ignorant, sometimes arrogant, young entrepreneur just trying to figure out his way in the vast jungle known as life.

I jumped from business to business, industry to industry, and every time I hated it because I felt like I was backtracking on my hard work. In retrospect, I didn't lose any time because I was more effective at the tasks that mattered. In every new endeavor I used the skills I learned in the one prior. To my surprise, I didn't lose the people who were following me because they were connecting and supporting

Isaac; not the professional I was working to become. Sure, I lacked the expertise and experience, but there was a deeper resonance with who I am as an individual. The fact that I was always seen drinking too much coffee, that I loved being out in nature and traveling. People saw that private side of me and when I got involved in the personal branding industry and began diving deeper and honing into my craft, I started to attract people who were there for the value they could receive.

There is a nuanced relationship between the person and the professional. I would make the argument that if you're just starting and don't know the figurative difference between up and down, you have a considerable advantage over the person who has years of experience and all of the degrees.

You're able to document your process from startup founder to owner of a booming business. The model who went from local magazines to international fashion shows. The comedian who performed at the smallest of comedy clubs to headlining Madison Square Gardens. The small town landscaper who started with a trailer hitched to their bike who now has a fleet of trucks. The author who began with short stories on the internet to books lining stores around the globe.

If you can show the *crunchiness* and *dirtiness* of starting and share your lessons along the way, there is a home-field advantage. You are doing the things that might not be sexy, *but are real*. A deep appreciation surrounds you and you'll have more credibility regardless of not having expertise. By the time you are ready to launch that product or take your performances to loftier levels, there will be a crowd of supporters cheering you on and saying that they had a part in your success— "I *knew them before they hit it big time.*"

Arguably, there are more lessons in showing failures and mistakes than there are in retroactively sharing stories that might not be relevant for today's world. Do not be discouraged by your lack of authority or experience. Have fun with your personal brand as there's a lot of work for you to do.

Q: Do you believe you have the experience or expertise to build in public? If not, what is your reasoning? After reading this subchapter do you feel more assured to move forward?

8.3 | Reinvesting Into Your Personal Brand

Do not expect your personal brand to generate a direct financial return for the first several years of conscious effort. There are some anomalies like those who are specifically growing their personal brand to drive sales for their businesses. The same can be said for the person who tweaks their own to earn a higher-paying position in a company. *These are exceptions but are not the rule.*

Fortunately, most of the investments that you do have to make into your personal brand are complementary to how you're already living. If you spend more money on the nicer phone instead of buying the cheaper one, you have a perfectly good camera for taking photos and recording video content. You likely have a desktop or laptop you use for work or play, and that's all you need to start. As you get more serious and create more content, you might consider investing in a home studio setup such as: lighting, a microphone, sound-proofing, tripod etc; to at least create structure and deliver consistent quality. If you're a blogger or write articles for publications, you may purchase software licenses to improve grammar and writing.

Your investments become a part of the infrastructure of your *"business."* Investing in your personal brand is having somebody help you with copywriting, paying a designer, taking a trip for an event, and even your personal growth through self-development books, coaching, courses and programs. In time you may consider forming an actual legal entity for your personal brand to offer an increased amount of protection and security for your privacy, tax benefits, and to boost your credibility. This is not a requirement, but it does provide more legitimacy.

A physical office space is not required as you can work out of your home or your favorite coffee shop, but if you find that it boosts your productivity the choice is ultimately your own. I use Mashman Consulting Group's physical office location for content creation, have access to complementary conference rooms, and I've seen a huge boost in my own efficiency. The amount of investment that you choose to make into your personal brand is relative to where you are in your brand's progression and career.

Don't be discouraged by a lack of funding or resources, instead, view it as a challenge you are willing to take on. The business professional who chooses to write a book is not going to make a lot of money directly through the publication of their work. It is in how they leverage their book that they can recoup their initial investment—many investments share a similar nature.

You're playing a game that doesn't have a finish line and a *scarcity mindset* keeps you in place. Take a few calculated risks! This is not financial advice recommending you pay $10,000 for some *"high-ticket coach"* but spending a few hundred or even a few thousand dollars on consultants and equipment to make you more proficient is usually worth it. Your current place is also not an indicator of your future; recognize that what might be a lot of money to you today is only a drop in the ocean for somebody else.

T: Write a list of all of the potential investments you may consider making. At what moment will you know when it's time to expend capital?

8.4 | **Building A Team**

Your personal brand is a business and must be treated as such. As a business grows so does its team. If your personal brand is generating money and is farther along when compared to a year or two ago, it might be time to assemble a team. These team members are not going to be formally employed in the *American W-2* sense, but will act as independent contractors that cultivate results in less time. You might hire a virtual assistant to scour the web and SAAS platforms for media opportunities or respond to small inquiries. You might bring on an agent who can help attract and close deals in a timely fashion. You may direct revenue toward campaign managers, coaches, copywriters, email newsletter specialists, graphic designers, photographers and videographers.

There are two main reasons why you would consider expanding your personal brand's team. First, is to refine your actions so you're spending time on tasks that pertain to your talent and expertise, and second, is to increase the quality of production for the things you are already creating. Because you can do something yourself doesn't mean you need to, especially if the byproducts can be better.

When I concluded that I wanted to become a professionally paid public speaker, I brought on a booking agent who gets a percentage cut of every deal he closes; within 60 days he landed a five-figure opportunity. The nuance is that you must, to some degree, have an already established reputation that makes representing you appear as a win-win. Building a team for your personal brand is not about taking things off your plate so you can slack off, it's about giving you the room to enter into *full-blown expansion mode*. Assign tasks that you're not good at, are particularly time-consuming, or you do not want to do. The more established your personal brand becomes, the more you can delegate and truth be told, the more people will want to work for and with you.

Q: Relating to tasks for your personal brand, A) What aren't you great at, and B) What are time-consuming tasks that you can outsource? Building your team is as much about resulting in better-end products as it is saving you time so you can focus on high-impact action.

8.5 | **Use Cases of Personal Branding**

Many of the examples we've covered have been aimed at entrepreneurs and sole–proprietors, but don't mistake personal branding as one-sided. Personal branding applies to the intrapreneur who works within a business as does it applies to the corporate professional who finds themself in a traditional 9-to-5 position. Executives go out of their way to improve their literal résumé through means such as certifications, furthering their education, and volunteer experience, and are working to build their personal brand in the hopes of asking for more and finding a job that they can make a career out of.

Mission-oriented school teachers can inspire legions of new teachers through their messaging while impacting the lives of hundreds of students. Charity programs led by public leaders attract more donations because of their ability to tell stories. The college athlete wanting to land a spot in the big leagues compiles highlight reels and uses their personal brand to get scouted for multimillion-dollar contracts fresh out of their senior year.

Personal branding is the very fabric of humanity and those who move from the Unconscious Incompetent [1.8] to being in conscious control, surpass their competitors by leaps and bounds. For those of you interested in landing that dream position, don't you think applying the principles we've discussed will give you a competitive advantage? Crafting an omnipresent personal brand may be the very thing that puts you in the crosshairs of decision-makers. Hiring someone who is self-sufficient and is actively making an effort to expand their capabilities is a decision that requires little thought. You'll eventually be presented with chances to represent your company that experienced employees aren't being chosen for. It's about putting yourself and your prowess into the spotlight. Is there anything inherently wrong with being the teacher's pet or the boss' favorite?

Business owners benefit the most from their personal brands more than any other example that I've given thus far. I would not have any of my current successes if it weren't for the conscious direction and action regarding my personal brand. The small business owner can build a multi-million or even billion-dollar company by becoming a public figure and subject matter expert. Many of the current marketing channels are completely free to use. One hundred years ago if a company wanted to reach consumers across the United States, they had to install entire electrical grids and lay down phone lines. Today you can pick up your phone, and in 60 seconds record a video and have provided access to nearly all of the developed civilization.

I adhere to the idea that an expert is obligated to share their expertise. A master tradesman mentors and offers guidance to the apprentice and journeyman. Traditionally, methodology and skills have been passed down through word-of-mouth and direct experience. Building in public as they say is multifaceted as it does not only educate people who are interested in your field professionally speaking, but also positively impacts the public via interesting tidbits of information, solutions, etc.

The business owner sets the example and shows that it is possible to go from a one-man shop to a booming corporation, meanwhile through their content and efforts, are attracting more business to their establishment. If you have the option to purchase from two companies, the first of which you only know for their services, whereas the second you know the owner, which one would you be more likely to support? *Emotions are what drives purchasing decisions.* The duty of providing a quality experience remains the same and long-term relationships end up more fulfilling.

Steve Jobs, despite being dead for many years, is attributed to the monumental achievements of Apple. The musical halls, museums, institutions, and theaters we visit are named after business moguls like John D. Rockefeller and Andrew Carnegie. In school, we learned about how Henry Ford produced the Model T car and changed how to this day, civilization commutes; how he influenced the industrialization of manufacturing. It is in the shadow of giants that we live, both good and bad. A business owner who decides to build in public is more likely to produce than the person nobody knows and who builds in private. *The commodity of influence is more important than the commodity itself.*

Q: What kind of student were you in high school or college? Did you notice any changes in your performance or opportunities made available to you?

8.6 | **Pivoting**

Who you are today is much different than who you were a decade ago. The idea of change and how it affects your personal brand isn't something to be fearful of. Instead, embrace it and respect the tremendous opportunity ahead of you to *Pivot*. With experience and time, your career and interest will change. Progression is a representation of executed action is it not? To date, I've pivoted several different times and in doing so, I always redirected *what I was promoting to match what I wanted to be known for.* I went from the industry of Network Marketing to working in the podcast industry, managing musical talent and building a record label, to building a public relations firm, and now consulting through Mashman Consulting Group.

Understanding what you deeply enjoy and what you want to do occupationally, requires leaps of faith and changing directions. I do not see myself having to make another pivot for quite some time, but 10 years from now who knows? I doubt that I'll become a Michelin Star Chef or make my debut as a professional athlete, but I do plan on using my work in personal branding to become a more rounded business figure who invests in commercial real estate and startups, and launch a series of new businesses. As I do, I plan on pivoting my marketing to move away from the personal branding expert, to that of a magnate.

As I mentioned in previous subchapters, I had wonderful people who continued to support me despite my professional pivots as they were connected with *Isaac*. Developing trust with your fanbase gives you the security to take those leaps and change directions. If you're embarking on a wonderful new career, you'll want to adjust your brand's messaging, your marketing materials, and the stories you tell while being interviewed. Use your experiences as building blocks integrated into what you share. Talk about how being a salesman for top companies led you to launch your own sales agency or how being a college athlete influenced you to pursue nonprofit work for the youth. Share your experience of being a defendant lawyer turned prosecutor—the public will support you if you give them a reason to.

You are not trapped in your current pursuits and do not be fearful of how people might respond. Making a notable pivot is an opportunity to promote something entirely new! Long gone is the age of pensions and jobs that people spend 40 years of their lives building. This is not an endorsement telling you to change pathways every other week, but from a branding and marketing standpoint relative to your personal brand, pivoting is something that in retrospect I miss doing because of how entertaining it was to transition my image and pursue positioning myself as an *"evolved"* version.

A: Begin operating with the confidence in knowing that should you need to figuratively *"start over"* you would be able to appropriately pivot your personal brand.

8.7 | **Establishing Personal Brand Habits**

As you add new aspects to your personal brand, the degree of necessary effort will accordingly increase. When you decide to commit to a weekly episode of your podcast or vlog, launch a newsletter, or post daily content, it requires you to show up and deliver. *Establishing Personal Brand Habits* is vital for the maintenance of momentum and the increase in results therein. If you choose to adopt *The Power of 3 [6.5]*, which calls for you to connect with three new people every single day, you won't see massive returns if you only employ it a couple of days at a time. It is only after a significant passage of time that your network begins to compound.

As professionals check their inbox every morning with their cup of coffee, responding to your messages and texts is similar. The habits that you choose to adopt for your personal brand will vary based on the methods you choose to employ. If you're a lifestyle influencer that relies on content creation to drive brand deals and generate affiliate income, it means every single day you should be documenting your life and creating content, or once or twice a week you need to sit down and create all of your content at once. It is then up to you and you alone to post daily or schedule it in advance. The public speaker will want to make a habit of posting clips from recent speeches and promoting them. The health coach who posts tips on how to get into better shape must adopt the same attitude with posting that they do in showing up to the gym. The timeframe for your personal branding habits vary based on the strategies you choose to employ.

You will dial in and find what works best for you and your schedule through trial and error. Getting busy and feeling like you don't have the bandwidth to show up is understandable, but in these moments, remind yourself of why you are building your personal brand to begin with. Is your temporary laziness worth sacrificing your ambitions? Why would you choose not to do something that could affect all of the momentum you've developed up until this point?

Get into a groove of sorts so small actions become second nature. An example from my own personal brand would be taking photos every time I get dressed up, recording a video as ideas cross my mind, and talking to strangers when I go to the store. These micro-habits contribute to the macro-picture. It's not about showing up when you feel motivated to, that's not where the genius lies. The genius lies in showing up when you don't feel like it as *your personal brand's results are apathetic to your times of weakness*.

On the same note as weakness, whatever the reasons are behind choosing not to take advantage of opportunities as they're presented to you, such as finding out about it too late, conflicts in readiness, or your inability to be receptive to new things, dwelling on missed opportunities is the equivalent of beating yourself up for not investing in a stock in the 1990s. Nothing that you could do and no amount of time spent dwelling on these passed over opportunities will ever change the fact that you missed them.

I have missed out on opportunities to gain enormous amounts of short-term exposure. I am specifically referring to new social media platforms coming onto the scene. Rather than spending my energy exerted towards exploiting adolescent algorithms, I missed my window. *So what; what has passed, has passed*. After learning these lessons, I have gotten better at identifying prospective platforms, understanding algorithms, and appreciating the frontier horizon that is the early days of new social networks.

Missing an opportunity for your personal brand might come in the form of not connecting with a person whilst you were face-to-face. You may have been exhausted because of your trip, felt under the weather, were too shy and lacked the courage to go up to them, or simply weren't in the state of mind to network. What good is beating yourself up? *Absolutely nothing.* Our mentality does not like losing, which is wonderful, but if you let your lack of previous action lead you down a path of procrastination, you will just lose out on more present-day opportunities. It's rudimentary to even discuss this, but in my time working with clients, it's not uncommon for them to talk about their missed opportunities.

T: Write out all of the obligations you have for your personal brand in its present state and curate a list of habits you need to adopt to take your progression to a more desired place.

8.8 | **Maintaining Relevance**

Momentum is easier kept than it is cultivated and it is easier to maintain relevance than it is trying to become relevant. Everything we have covered in this book is intended to give you a steady foundation that you can quickly build upon. You want your personal brand to be structurally sound and organized enough that you are in control of the perception around you, can proficiently direct resources, and spend time performing the tasks conducive to your future. There is no point in experimenting to find what works and what doesn't when you can get all of the lessons ahead of time.

The first couple of years of purposefully building your personal brand are the most challenging. Once your momentum is established and at least several hundred people know about you, what you're building, who you are, etc; you can mobilize these individuals like a general does in wartime to become your largest advocates and promoters.

To once again use the example of a corporation, they do not become billion-dollar grossing companies off of their marketing alone. It is through distribution channels and the word-of-mouth of their consumers that they become household names with their products lining the shelves of our stores and their services our go-to. It isn't a coincidence that I compare your personal brand to that of a company brand. Nearly everything a corporation has to do, you have to do for your personal brand.

Without showing up everyday how can you ever expect to maintain the momentum you worked so hard to develop? Think of the example of a snowball rolling downhill. I've never tried this myself, but it is a common example we see in cartoons and use in our analogous language. It starts with one snowball the size of your hand and as it rolls downhill, it grows and has more force behind it. If it never stops, it continues to grow. Momentum can be seen in a social media algorithm that uses mathematical equations to determine what posts to push out and what posts do not deserve more exposure. If a post gets enough engagement in the first several hours of its life, it's indicative that it is worth being promoted. It then gets pushed out to more accounts who share some degree of curiosity or interest in the subject matter, and if it appeals to enough people, it goes out to the masses.

Unlike a viral post, the likelihood that your personal brand becomes a viral sensation overnight is very low and it's halfwitted to rely on virality for your success. Momentum is built over an extended period and is combined with dedicated actions. As long as your community is able to see that you are in the pursuit of a larger goal or vision, they will stay engaged and be less likely to become fatigued. *Refer to Audience Fatigue [5.12] for further reference.* It is when you slow down and stop performing the habits for your personal brand, the momentum you sought so dearly after begins to drop.

Relevancy on the other hand is directly tied to a person's degree of momentum. The more momentum your personal brand has, the more relevant you will be in the minds of others. The less conversation that surrounds you in public, the less relevancy you'll have in private. If people are only talking about you when you post something, they won't be privately conversing about you. How many situations have you been in where you were talking with a friend about celebrity gossip or a musician's album and the subject at hand wasn't in the room with you? You're a factor in that person's momentum and your conversations are keeping them relevant! An advocate for somebody who doesn't even know you... This is a prefatory reflection of what others need to be doing for you and in order for this to happen, it befalls your shoulders to give them valid reasons to.

Q: Who is a celebrity that has *"lost their luster?"* What led to this person's collapse in relevancy and what could they have avoided?

8.9 | **The Future of Personal Branding**

What is *The Future of Personal Branding?* I believe that there isn't one singular answer as it is reliant on personal opinion, societal factors, and technology but for the most part, I anticipate the idea of conscious personal branding becoming more practiced and widely accepted. Being an influencer will be appreciated and viewed as a genuine way of making a living by people both young and old, employees will understand the impact that their personal brands' footprint has on their careers, and traditionally private corporate executives will choose to face the public head on outside of making public appearances as they address crises or boost their stock prices. Small business owners will go out of their way to position themselves as experts and public figures. Politicians are going to be required to speak with more transparency and live up to their promises.

The public's awareness and ability to snuff out scammers and less-than-do-good characters will become heightened and our society as a whole will continue to operate with influence as a currency. The argument could be made that a society so driven by influence and perceptions may lead to an Orwellian world or one that is based on a social credit score. This shares similarities with those who make the argument that artificial intelligence will give rise to evil and oppressive robotic overlords. *The social credit score already exists.* Our personal credit score determines what houses we can buy, cars we can drive, and the loans we qualify for. The way we dress impacts perceptions and how people treat us. The number in our bank account opens up a door full of glamour and more expensive realities, concurrently changing how people treat us. The number of followers we have on social media produces psychological biases on how others view us. *Essentially, your personal brand is your social credit score.*

The technologies that come about in the coming decades are worth mentioning but it's preposterous to think that we can predict at what magnitude they will impact us. In the last several years, artificial intelligence has gone from only being used in robotics and military operations to becoming publicly accessible in the form of image generators, large language models, video editors, and AI-based search engines. I had the opportunity to contribute a quote for a notable publication on the subject

"Will AI replace consultants?" My opinion was and remains the same, that AI will enhance a consultant's capabilities and lead to more resolute strategies. My reasoning behind this is reliant on mankind's ability to see and factor in emotions.

Humans have been and will remain emotional beings that are drawn to shiny objects and are attracted to the most suitable mates. We will always laugh at funny jokes or cry when a movie is sad. Human connection for as much as artificial intelligence might displace jobs or make reality appear more dystopian, will prevail.

The future of personal branding is becoming all the more fabricated. This is why the *Skyline Strategy* as covered in my paper *Identity Positioning [i]*, is not just a recommendation, it's a requirement for longevity. If everybody is trying to become somebody, you'll need to use every tool at your disposal to rise above and position yourself as that 1% figure. I am a believer in Adam Smith's concept of the Invisible Hand in reference to economics and I believe that there is a synonymous Invisible Hand that guides every person's sense of ambition.

This Manifesto provides you with nearly everything that is needed to have a successful personal brand and oversee your reputation, but if you do not execute on any of the provided strategies, don't expect miracles to happen. The future of personal branding is one of formidable competition.

Q: Where do you see the future of personal branding going? How will it impact, if at all, how you are branding and marketing yourself?

8.10 | **The Mask and the Mirror**

You don't build your personal brand based on what other people want to see, you build your personal brand because people come to you for *who you are*. You have the ability to build your personal brand in one of two ways. One is by putting on a mask that covers up your true self, and the other is by displaying the person you actually see in the mirror.

You should always do things for your personal brand that generate a net-positive, but that does not mean that everything you speak about is positive. Masquerading around as a perfect human who never makes mistakes is the opposite of vulnerable and prevents people from connecting with the true version of YOU. Harnessing aspects of your identity and highlighting your most positive traits may influence a person into thinking you're great, but adversely it also negates the benefits received from occasionally exposing your flaws.

The Mask of Perfection only causes you to hate the person staring back at you in the mirror that much more. This speaks to growing into the individual that you want to highlight for the rest of the world to see. You may be filled with doubt and suspicion in private and the public will be able to see right through it given enough time. Insecurities are part of the human experience and we all have them. Artists use their artwork to express themselves, and the thoughts that are passing through their mind as they make each brush stroke. Musicians tell their stories using microphones in the same way.

Consciously building your personal brand enables you to achieve nearly all of your business, financial, and personal goals.

If you still don't believe me this late into the book, I would challenge you to look beyond your immediate circle. Examine those that are successful. This *Philosophy of Personal Branding* applies in principle to every single person who has ever walked the face of this planet. From Pontious Pilate to Nero, Martin Luther King to Rosa Parks, the forgotten Mesopatamian farmer to the most well-known International Icon [1.8]. Look at the top figures of society. The sportscasters you follow, television anchors you trust to share the news, and movie stars you name your children after.

Aside from the fact they are all human and many have worked to get to the top of their fields, the one thing they all have in common is their personal brand. Your vision should be ever-growing and there will come a time when you meet many of your goals and what you thought was out of reach yesterday, becomes a present reality. When this happens expand your thinking and set your vision even farther out. You should be actively *chasing your vision*. To focus on your legacy while you're alive is to take away from the time you can spend actually building it. I used to live under the belief that my legacy was one of the most important parts of success, that is until the people around me who I cared about passed away.

Death became my acquaintance and it acted as my mentor. At funerals, I asked myself *"If I died tomorrow would I give a damn who showed up?"* Of course not...I'd be dead. Elvis Presley had a procession that went on for miles, but I bet he would have traded the largest funeral for another day on Earth, free of his contracts.

Your legacy is a result of your actions and accomplishments while you're alive. It's a combination of the way you made others feel, your laugh, your smile, your successes, and your moments of defeat. It's the experiences you live, the family you build, and the friends you make. The closest thing to the *"death"* of your personal brand, is being forgotten altogether. The childless person may not conceive a lineage, but they will be a part of someone else's. The more you contribute to society, the bigger the legacy. Understand this correlation and be comforted by it. Don't concern yourself with building a legacy—*become big enough the legacy is written for you.*

At the center of all achievement is personal growth and the best way of pursuing your vision comes by being intentional. Respect the contents within these pages. Use them ethically, morally, and with the right intentions. Do not use the psychological aspects to your gain if it ends in the downfall of another. There is more than enough for all of us.

My question to you is this. Are you building your personal brand to represent the Mask, or to represent the person who's staring back at you in the mirror?

| § |

Afterword

You would think that it would be impossible to summarize nearly 80 subchapters into one sentence, let alone one word, but I will. **YOU.**

Your personal brand is YOU. It is your gift and your curse. Your burden and your weapon. It is your individual reputation. It is what you will be building throughout the remainder of your life and what will exist long after your death. I understand that this book might not have been the strategic guide that addresses the current marketing channels available at the time of its publication in 2025, yet I assure you this was done intentionally. I never set out to write a lead magnet on how to post on a specific social media platform or structure an email message. I set out to write something based on empirical experience and observation. Something philosophical while also offering bursts of strategic insights.

The jump to the Second Edition from the First is incomprehensible. I essentially rewrote the entirety of the First Edition and expanded it by more than 10 times. I doubt that I will ever make a leap of this magnitude again. As for the Third Edition of *Personal Branding: Manifesto and Fame Influence* I cannot say when it is coming out but the intent has already been set. The next edition will be centered around moving from empirical to evidence-based and provide supporting case studies and research that this edition does not have. It is a growing body of work and there is no telling how many I will write in the coming years as I set out to prove and vindicate the world's *First Philosophy of Personal Branding.*

You can also expect the Third Edition to be broadened to apply to the general public and delve into specific use cases of how it applies not only to individuals driven by fame and influence, but to the local leader who wants to make an impact in their community or the teacher that wants to further their students' prospective future.

Throughout the Manifesto, I referenced many stories from my own career. My aim with the Editions to come is to share all the more grounded stories from others. These examples may come from clients of Mashman Consulting Group, interviews with well-regarded public figures, and projects that I fund.

I understand that this work would not be complete if I did not provide you with a proper way of measuring results with your personal brand. The avoidance of current marketing vehicles puts a slight limit on the specificity that I would otherwise provide to my clients, but in general, you will *feel* the results of your personal brand. What took you years to accomplish, may only take months, weeks, or even days. You will feel your credibility being bolstered by an influx of commendations and recommendations from those around you that you endear and respect. The publications you once set out to be featured in, may be approaching you for quotes and will come at such a rate that you could be published multiple times in the same year as I was.

The number of people who comment on your social media posts or sign up for your offers will drastically increase. The rate at which you close your business prospects may become so high you have too many clients to work with. The deals that come your way and the amount of publicity may make you feel uncomfortable and out of place at times. The conversations that surround your name and the circles in which your name is mentioned might just be in entirely different socioeconomic classes. You will wake up one morning and see that your material was used in another person's content without you even knowing that they ever set out to promote it. Measuring the results of your personal brand is as much in feeling as it is the exact measurement of engagement rates, follower counts, referrals from supporters, and the commas in your bank account.

At times, measuring your personal brand's results will not be wholly positive. After a controversial statement, an extended break, or a less-than-endearing aspect of your life becoming public, you may find yourself thinking about sections of my Manifesto. Your engagement could drop, your audience could shrink, and your reputation tarnished. It is, after all, a double-edged sword that can cut in the right places, but can also cut you, if it's not properly handled. Alternatively, a platform that you rely on for marketing may change their algorithm and you find yourself not with a smaller audience, but instead an audience that has a hard time finding you. This is another reason I chose to remain agnostic from hard mentions of specific platforms and focus on omnipresence instead.

Every person who reads this book is trying to build a personal brand that is entirely different from that of every other. Civilization has brought about new technological advancements but the nature of man has largely remained the same. We seek to be appreciated and ask others for validation. Whereas we no longer have Kings and Queens who rule off of Divine Rights, we have Presidents and Parliamentary Members we put our trust in. Instead of visiting the Roman Colosseum to watch Gladiators, we visit stadiums to see our favorite sports teams play.

Take what I wrote in the chapter *Reputation Management [5]*, especially close to heart as with more power and influence, the cockier you might find yourself becoming. You could find yourself thinking that you're too good for certain conversations. You may find yourself on a big yacht, but you should never be too big to take out the small boat with some friends.

As with all philosophical works, the greatest value will come through introspection and reflection. Not once was I trying to hide any information between the lines, but some statements are more profound than others. This is not a manual that focuses on micro subjects and I would dare say that this is more along the lines of a religious text that shares a macroscopic way of living.

With the Third Edition, I'll be bringing proof and expanding on how this *Philosophy of Personal Branding* applies to every single person, regardless of how large or small their chief aim may be.

Hold me to this promise.

Your personal brand when consciously built can be a force for good or a force for destruction.

> - Isaac Mashman

Isaac's Step-by-Step Personal Branding Process

Step 1: *Define Your Personal Brand & Develop Your Core Mindset*

- Answer the *4 Pillar Questions [1.7]* to establish the foundation of your brand:
    1. *Why do you want to build your personal brand?*
    2. *What do you want to be known for?*
    3. *Who are you?*
    4. *How do you get to where you want to be?*
- Avoid clichés *[4.5]* and lean into your unique name, persona, and skills.
- Define your intent and create a Code of Conduct *[5.10]—what do you want your brand to stand for?*
- Shift your mindset from short-term thinking to a life-long commitment *[3.1]*.

Step 2: *Position Yourself Strategically (Identity Positioning Framework)*

- Merge your personal and professional identity to create a cohesive personal brand *[6.3]*.
- Craft your Elevator Pitch *[4.3]*—a short and memorable statement that summarizes who you are and what you do.
- Build a seamless and consistent image across all platforms, from social media to in-person interactions *[4.16]*.
- Optimize your messaging *[6.2]*:
  - Hook first, explain later—grab attention before diving into details.

Step 3: *Develop Your Personal Brand's Content & Network*

- Use The Power of 3 *[6.5]*:
  - Engage with three new people daily to expand your network.
- Diversify content formats *[i]*:
  - Text *(posts and thought-leadership)*
  - Audio *(podcasts, radio, interviews)*
  - Video *(vlogs, short videos, collaborations)*

Step 4: *Establish Habits & Master Distribution*

- Establish personal brand habits *[8.7]* (e.g., *content creation schedule, networking routines).*
- Set public goals and put forth a vision *[6.6]*—give your audience something to follow and support.
- Research ways to increase the distribution channels of your content and efforts *[6.11].*

Step 5: *Build Credibility & Your Reputation*

- Compile Wins *[5.14]*—showcase achievements to build authority *(features and interviews).*
- Manage risk and crisis *[5]*—be proactive in protecting your reputation.
- Give strategic *[5.11]*—align yourself with other credible figures.
- Reinvest in your brand *[8.3]*—invest time and money in your team, collaborations, new opportunities, and tools.
- Pivot and evolve when necessary *[8.6]*—update your materials, messaging, and efforts accordingly.

Acknowledgments

I want to take this time to thank the following people for helping me in the production and publication of my Second Edition. To Eric Chow, my friend, business partner, editor, and author of this book's foreword, thank you for your continued trust in me and our shared vision. You have exceeded my expectations time and time again and your help in the final weeks before publication cannot be understated. Alexander Stephens, my amazing designer and the creative genius who is visually helping me redefine my personal brand, your ideas with the cover design were and are remarkable. Your visually inclined eye was able to catch elements I hadn't even considered and I look forward to all we do together.

Mom, I know our relationship has gone through many changes and trials, but I am grateful for all of the sacrifices you made for me growing up and sheltering me from the things I used to criticize you on, that in retrospect I was too young to understand. I am grateful for your assistance in editing this book and being a part of something so meaningful to me. You were able to catch discrepancies and push my thinking in ways only *you* could. Grandma, as much as I wish you were alive to read this and see how far I have come, I know you would be proud. You listened to me for countless hours as I talked about not only my traumas but also my dreams. Papa, I thank you for teaching me how to use my hands, the importance of hard work and to be comfortable getting dirty. I miss those early mornings going to the cabinet shop and the late-night fish fries. I miss you both. Dad, if you asked me years ago if I ever would have thought we'd have a relationship, I'd have laughed out loud. I am grateful to know the man who gave me my last name and I'm greatly looking forward to building our relationship in the years to come and getting to know my brothers.

Hannah, my fiancée and partner in this mess called life, I love you and I thank you for continuing to support me and give me the runway to pursue my ambitions for our family and future. You have done more for me than I think you could ever realize and give me added reason to keep going. Kevin, my friend and adopted brother, I cherish our friendship more than anybody else's. You've encouraged me for well over a decade and have seen me at my most vulnerable moments. More importantly, you've always held me accountable. This thanks extends to your parents as I truly appreciate all they've done for me over the years.

To my various mentors, some who have since passed on: Bob Proctor, thank you for changing the way I think through your teachings. Earl Nightingale, the resounding radio host and early mentor to Bob, thank you for *The Strangest Secret* and breaking down why some who set out for success, never obtain it; *Man simply does not think.* I listened to this audio dozens of times, if not more and cannot name another that rivals in impact. Gary Vaynerchuk, although I have stopped closely following your content, without my introduction to your work in 2017 I doubt I would have ever picked up my outdated, second hand phone and recorded the first episode *The Isaac Mashman Show.* To Marvin Coffman aka *"Big Marv,"* the first client who showed me that I could charge more than $100 for my experience, you have continued to be a good friend and mentor to me, and your support has been unwavering. The final mentor I would like to acknowledge is Andy Frisella. I remember obsessively listening to nearly every episode of *The MFCEO Project* in 2018 as I was stocking shelves at my second job. Your virtual guidance and mentorship has been instrumental in shaping me into the man I am today and much of the chapter on *Mindset [3]* can be attributed, to some degree, to *you*. It was your criticisms on the internet space that influenced me to slow down and earn my titles. To stand out amongst the rest and become a leader who paves his own path and guides his family and friends. *I thank you more than most.*

It is through these people and numerous others that I don't have the space to include, have I been able to see some inkling of success and purpose in my goals. By reading this, you too are a part of my story and I thank you.

About The Author

Isaac Mashman is an American businessman, investor, podcast host, public speaker, and coffee addict, born in Jacksonville, Florida. In November 2021, he published *Personal Branding: A Manifesto on Fame and Influence*, which became Amazon's **#1 New Release in Public Relations** and a **top 10 best-seller** in the same category. Three years later, he returns with a fully expanded and revised Second Edition. As the founder of **Mashman Consulting Group**, a firm specializing in personal brand strategy for emerging and established public figures, Isaac is dedicated to defining this evolving field and setting the industry standard. He currently resides in **Little Rock, Arkansas**, with his fiancée, their two dogs, and four well-fed cats.

Contact Information

Website: isaacmashman.com
Social Media: @isaacmashman
Email: contact@isaacmashman.com

Work With Isaac Mashman

If you are interested in optimizing and scaling your personal brand and would like to book a consultation with Isaac Mashman, please reach out to Mashman Consulting Group by visiting their website *mashmancg.com*.

Book Isaac Mashman

If you're an event planner or host looking to hire Isaac Mashman for an upcoming event, please reach out to his team at *bookings@isaacmashman.com*. Isaac is available for conferences, fireside chats, full-day experiences, keynote presentations, summits, and Q&A sessions.

About the Publisher

Mashman Publishing is an exclusive imprint of *Mashman Consulting Group (MCG)*, created to publish works that align with the principles of business strategy, personal branding, and personal development. As a division of MCG, Mashman Publishing focuses on sharing insights that enable individuals to achieve measurable results and enhance their influence using their personal brands. All titles under Mashman Publishing are curated and published with the expertise and direction of Isaac Mashman.

Referenced Works

- Aesop. *The Hare and the Tortoise*. In *Aesop's Fables*. Greece: c. 600 BCE.
- Bernays, Edward. *Propaganda*. New York: Horace Liveright, 1928.
- Hill, Napoleon. *Think and Grow Rich*. Meriden, CT: The Ralston Society, 1937.
- Machiavelli, Niccolò. *The Prince*. Florence: Antonio Blado d'Asola, 1532.
- Orwell, George. *1984*. London: Secker & Warburg, 1949.
- Peters, Tom. *The Brand Called You. Fast Company*, 1997. [https://www.fastcompany.com/28905/brand-called-you/].
- Smith, Adam. *An Inquiry into the Nature and Causes of the Wealth of Nations*. London: W. Strahan and T. Cadell, 1776

INDEX

If you found the Second Edition of *Personal Branding: A Manifesto on Fame and Influence* helpful, I'd ask that you please consider leaving a review on the retailer you purchased it from. Your feedback helps others discover the world's first *Philosophy of Personal Branding* and begin consciously taking control of their own.

I appreciate the time that you spent reading my work in its entirety and would love to share in your accomplishments.

Please let me know how this Manifesto has helped you.

Much love,
Isaac Mashman